THE DEAD SEA SCROLLS

A New Historical Approach

THE
DEAD SEA SCROLLS

A New
Historical Approach

By CECIL ROTH

W · W · NORTON & COMPANY · INC · New York

FOREWORD

This book, first published in England six years ago, is the contribution of a professional historian to the solution of one of the most fascinating problems that has ever engaged the world of scholarship—that of the origin and background of the now famous Dead Sea Scrolls. My conclusions were derided at the time; and in order to clear up certain outstanding details I wrote a few subsidiary articles, among them those which figure as the Introduction and Appendices H and I of the present edition. When the excavations at the Zealot stronghold of Masadah began in the autumn of 1963, I felt that my case would be finally proved if a single document in any way analogous to the Qumran literature were to come to light there. But a document was found which exceeded all possible expectations on my part —a fragment of a remarkable liturgy considerable portions of which had already been found in the Qumran caves, and which was based on a curious method of calendrical computation used at Qumran. There was not the slightest rational doubt henceforth that my conjectures were correct. This book is accordingly reissued now, with additional materials, not only for its bearing on first century history but also as an exemplification of the validity of the historical method.

There is only one point on which there has been reason to modify my first conclusions. Originally I did not reexamine the prevailing view that the Teacher of Righteousness of the Qumran sect was put to death by his enemy, the Wicked Priest. Careful reading of the fragmentary 'pesher' on Psalms, with its jubilant celebration of the triumph of the righteous (there identified with the Teacher) made me realize that this was unlikely. Hence the Teacher of Righteousness (a title prompted by Joel 2:23 and bestowed on the person believed to be the Ultimate Leader at the End of Days) was in all probability the leader of the Forlorn Hope at Masadah. His enemy, the Wicked Priest, is certainly a leader of the Priestly Faction which so frenziedly opposed the *Sicarii* and Zealots during the Jewish Revolution, but I am now less inclined to identify him with any specific individual active at the time.

These details, however, are immaterial. The essential is that, after two thousand years, we now find ourselves in the possession of the patriotic literature which inspired the most uncompromising of the participants in the great Jewish Revolt against the Romans in 66–73. No literary discovery of the past generation can approach this in importance.

CECIL ROTH

Jerusalem, Israel
March 5, 1965

CONTENTS

CHRONOLOGICAL TABLE FOR
THE HISTORY OF THE ZEALOTS AND QUMRAN SECT

B.C.

46	Hezekiah's revolt suppressed by Herod, and Hezekiah is executed.
31	*Earthquake destroys Qumran.*
4	Judah ben Hezekiah's revolt at Sepphoris, which is recaptured by the Romans and sacked; *Judah and his followers find refuge in Damascus?*

A.D.

4–6	Judah introduces Zealot ideas into Judaea.
	Qumran reoccupied.
	Revolt and death of Judah.
46–8	Execution of Jacob and Simon ben Judah.
	Menahem ben Judah becomes head of the sect.
52–60	Sicarii begin activity.
66	Menahem seizes Masadah.
	Menahem takes command in Jerusalem and defeats Romans.
66 (Sept.)	Menahem goes to the Temple and is assassinated by priestly party; his kinsman Eleazar leads his followers back to Dead Sea area.
67?	Simon bar Giora joins Zealots at Masadah but subsequently leaves them.
67 (Passover)	Zealots storm Engedi.
68 (June)	Vespasian captures Jericho and visits Dead Sea.
70 (summer)	Fall of Jerusalem.
?	Fall of Herodium and Machaerus.
73	Fall of Masadah and death of Eleazar ben Jair.
	Repression of Zealots in Egypt and Cyrene.
114/5–7	Zealot revolts in Egypt, Cyrene, Mesopotamia, Cyprus.

INTRODUCTION

Until a very short while ago, the origin of the Dead Sea Scrolls seemed destined to remain one of the insoluble mysteries of history—at least so far as a small minority of skeptics was concerned, for majority opinion aligned itself very early and never saw any reason why its comfortable conclusions should be disturbed. The Scrolls first came to light in 1947 in a cave near the northern end of the Dead Sea, and further finds were subsequently made in similar repositories in the same region. In this area also there were excavated in due course the remains of a nexus of buildings apparently adapted to a sort of group-living arrangement, to which the documents presumably bore some connection. According to the writings of Pliny, the west bank of the Dead Sea was in the 1st century the center of the Essenes, the unworldly Jewish monastic sect who, because of the light they and their doctrines throw on the origins of Christianity, have attracted so much attention from historians of religion. Since the findings on the west bank of the Dead Sea obviously pertained to an ascetic sect dating back to the same period, it seemed equally obvious that what had been so amazingly discovered was the basic literature of the Essenes.

The key figure to emerge from the Scrolls as the leader and, as it were, prophet of the sect is designated the Teacher of Righteousness. This personage appears in a series of Biblical glosses discovered among the Scrolls, the most remarkable being a kind of commentary on the Book of Habakkuk which formed part of the original cache, and which is preserved almost in its entirety. We are given a good deal of information about the Teacher in various respects, but one episode stands out above all: how he was at loggerheads with 'the Wicked Priest,' apparently the representative of 'official' Judaism at the time; how this same Wicked Priest was sent against him on the holy Day of Atonement to 'swallow him up' (whether in a physical or spiritual sense, or whether this implies that the Teacher was

xi

killed, is not quite clear); and how God intervened to save him in due course. This episode seems to have been the sect's central historical experience (the Scrolls are full of allusions to it, direct or indirect), and scholars have accordingly been busily engaged in attempting to identify it and the principal persons involved.

One elaborate theory—which greatly excited uninformed opinion—located the episode in the pre-Christian period: the saintly Teacher of the sect was first persecuted by his enemies, then put to death by them (it was even added 'by crucifixion,' though this was nowhere stated, and though it is even doubtful whether the Teacher's persecution had a fatal outcome), and subsequently raised from the dead (because the Scrolls say at one point that God will 'raise up' the Teacher of Righteousness at the 'end of days'). In short, here, it seemed, was the basic Christian story in the literature of a Jewish sect which was believed to have flourished one or two centuries before the birth of Jesus. It is this sensational possibility rather than the real scientific or historical or literary interest of the documents which has been largely responsible for the widespread interest of the general public in the subject.

My own conclusions, diametrically opposed to this and based on purely historical reasoning, will be found in the following pages. The only thing that mystified me was why something so obvious had not been realized before, and by scholars far better qualified than I am to work upon this period. When, however, I published the preliminary results of my investigation, my views were greeted not merely with disagreement but with almost universal derision. To my amazement, I found that in the circles dealing with this period and this subject there obtained a standard of language and conduct, as well as of research, the like of which I had never experienced in my career as a historian. I may cite as characteristic a statement by a Professor Sandmel, which was seized upon and quoted with gusto by other critics. My hypothesis, said the professor, 'wins by a length . . . the race for the most preposterous of the theories about the Scrolls.' Most of the 'learned' periodicals did not even trouble to notice the book at all, the sales were negligible, and my theories did not make the slightest impact. Meanwhile work after work on the Scrolls continued to appear, still based on the old and certainly untenable (whether or not my own views were correct) Essene hypothesis. Some even contained maps of the area copiously indicating the purported location of the Essene settlements!

With very few exceptions, even those who did me the courtesy of reading my book did not think it worthwhile to reply seriously to arguments that they considered wholly fantastic. So far as any rebuttals were made at all, they were sporadic and to a great extent inconsequential. These reactions may have been due, I fear, to resentment (not always unconscious) at the intrusion of a medievalist into this specialized field. As one highly respected American archaeologist remarked, my book showed the dangers of trying to solve such problems on the basis of history alone. A curious criticism, it seems to me, for do not the same methods of historical investigation apply to all periods?

More reasoned opposition was advanced by Father de Vaux in his celebrated Schweich lectures delivered before the British Academy in 1959, and subsequently published. But here, too, the historian found himself in a new world where the scholarly standards and methods to which he was accustomed evidently did not apply. For Father de Vaux postulated quite arbitrarily that none of the documents found in the Dead Sea caves could have been composed after the destruction of the monastic center at Qumran—this notwithstanding the discovery there of the copper scrolls listing the Temple treasure, which it is universally agreed are posterior to that event. When, then, in Father de Vaux's opinion, was Qumran destroyed? On the evidence of a token of the Tenth Legion which was discovered at Qumran, and on the basis of the assertion that according to Josephus, Vespasian advanced in the summer of 68 with the Tenth Legion from Caesarea down the Jordan valley and reached Jericho, near Qumran—Father de Vaux asked whether it was not self-evident that the token was mislaid at Qumran at this time, thus fixing precisely, almost within weeks, the date of the center's capture by the Romans. None of the Dead Sea documents could therefore be later than this period, the summer of 68. Consulting Josephus, however, we find that in the campaign in question Vespasian did *not* march from Caesarea; his line of advance was *not* down the Jordan valley; and he did *not* have with him the Tenth Legion, then on special duty elsewhere! In addition, it subsequently transpired that what had been identified as a token of the Legion was in fact a coin of Ascalon of a later date which had been wrongly identified.

Another argument brought up against me was that my assumption that Masadah and Qumran belonged to the same geographical area was erroneous. A fair distance separates the two, as well as almost insuperable natural barriers, and hence— so I was told—it is out of the question that there could have been any close association between the two centers. However, during the past couple of years, legal documents from Masadah of a somewhat later date have been discovered in the Qumran area, so that this argument (for what it was worth) automatically collapsed. And, as we shall see presently, there is now the most positive evidence of close association between the two centers.

My critics have also raised other objections. If the Qumran sect did, in fact, exist in the period of the war against the Romans of 66–73, why were they so bitterly opposed to the revolutionary leaders? Why did they not march to the relief of the Holy City in its agony in the spring and early summer of the year 70? These arguments, however, present no problem at all, for my postulate concerning the leaders of the Qumran sect corresponds in any case with Josephus's description of the *Sicarii* of Masadah. Besides, the line of conduct pursued by the Qumran leaders must seem to the student of history natural enough, for it accords perfectly with standard revolutionary and, indeed, sectarian psychological patterns. The extreme revolutionary wing invariably accuses the more moderate one in due course of counter-revolutionary tendencies; the original leaders are then frequently discarded and in many cases switch back their allegiance and 'betray the revolution'; a wave of terror often follows, inspired by the purest of motives, and sometimes implemented by the most spiritual of demagogues, against those who were once idols of the people. The scene as I reconstructed it appeared paradoxical, if not incredible, to my philologist or archaeologist critics. But to any student interested in the history of sectarianism or the history of revolution, it is absolutely logical and even, one might say, inevitable.

The basic objection to my views, however, whether expressed or not, and the one which caused them to be characterized as wholly preposterous, stemmed from my suggestion that the God-intoxicated sect whose literature has survived in the Dead

Sea Scrolls was actually the Zealots, the bloodthirsty political extremists so unfavorably depicted in the pages of Josephus. In this crucial divergence, the importance of the mere historical approach becomes apparent. For what the non-historian could not recognize was that Josephus was employing all the standard counter-revolutionary commonplaces invoked by their enemies against revolutionaries in whatever era: that they are immoral, godless, corrupt, and love destruction for its own sake. What Josephus said about the Zealots of his day is no different from what was said about the fathers of the French Revolution and the Russian Revolution and the American Revolution and the English Revolution of the 17th century. It is similar to what was said in the communiqués of the German High Command about the resistance movements in France and Italy and Poland during World War II.

Elsewhere, however, Josephus makes it clear that the Zealots (or rather the *Sicarii*) were far from being mere political extremists and advocates of violence. He includes them among the various religious sects into which the Jewish people were divided in his day, by the side of the Essenes and the Sadducees and the Pharisees. He also indicates the basis of their distinctive theological outlook—the dogma that it was a mortal sin to admit any sovereignty over the Jewish people but the sovereignty of God. From this dogma, the rest followed ineluctably—both the Romans and those Jewish leaders who advocated submission to the Romans must be disposed of by whatever means, including assassination.

The political intransigence of the Zealots was thus implicit in their religious doctrine, even as their implacable violence was a logical consequence of their all-embracing religious dogma. Moreover, the essentially doctrinal rather than merely political nature of this sect is quite clearly suggested by Josephus when he alludes to the successive leaders, Judah and Menahem (and presumably the latter's successor Eleazar ben Jair as well) as *sophistae* or teachers. It is true that Josephus nowhere explicitly states that the *Sicarii* followed any distinctive religious practices as the Qumran sect apparently did (especially in the matter of the religious calendar), but there was no particular reason why he should have. Except as regards the Essenes, whose ascetic organization had a certain publicity value for his purpose, Josephus precisely delineates only the characteristics which differentiated the sects from one another—in the case of the *Sicarii*, for example, their insistence on the exclusive sovereignty of God over the Jewish people. A moment's consideration, however, is enough to tell us that this doctrine itself must have implied certain variant religious practices—for example, the prohibition (referred to in the New Testament) against using money bearing the likeness of the Roman emperor. On the one hand, nothing in the code of the Qumran sect is at variance with what we know of the *Sicarii*-Zealot religious observance; on the other, it is possible to say positively that the Qumran sect can be identified neither with the Essenes nor the Pharisees nor the Sadducees as those groups are described by Josephus. Unless there existed yet another group of which we have no record whatsoever, then, the sect in question must have been the Zealots—the only contemporary body against which, at least so far as the religious issue is concerned, there is at all events no contrary evidence.

Nothing, it seemed to me, could challenge the validity of this historical reasoning, but it seemed equally clear that nothing could have any impact on those unable to follow it—except the emergence of new evidence that would decide the matter incontrovertibly. Such evidence has now, I am happy to say, come to light, and the result is that the mystery of the Dead Sea Scrolls is no longer a mystery.

During the winter of 1963-4, Professor Yadin of the Hebrew University in Jerusalem undertook, in his usual superbly organized fashion, a campaign of excavation at Masadah, a hitherto imperfectly explored site. Masadah is situated at the summit of an almost unscalable hill overhanging the western bank of the Dead Sea, about thirty miles south of Qumran, where the bulk of the Scrolls were found. The late Hasmonaeans constructed a fortress there, which was transformed by Herod the Great into a luxurious palace. (Josephus describes this structure in minute detail, and his description had been confirmed point for point in the course of earlier excavations, even before Yadin began his operations.) On the death of Herod, the Romans converted the palace into a garrison-fortress which was used to overawe the neighboring terrain. In the spring or summer of 66, the stronghold was captured by Menahem ben Judah at the head of the *Sicarii*, who equipped themselves from its lavish arsenal before marching on Jerusalem. After Menahem's assassination that autumn, his nephew and successor, Eleazar ben Jair, withdrew to the fortress with his surviving followers; repulsed successive expeditions sent from Jerusalem to quell them; joined for a time with other extremists only to quarrel with them soon after; extended his hold on the surrounding area; carried out forays both against isolated Roman forces and against villages which had remained loyal to the Provisional Revolutionary Government in the capital; and continued to glower defiance at the outside world from his impregnable fortress, his hand against every man and every man's hand against him. In all this, Eleazar and his followers were obviously buoyed up by the belief endemic to religious revolutionaries everywhere—that only when God's will was made supreme and their internal opponents overthrown would they be able to triumph over their external enemies and the 'end of days' foretold in prophecy be brought to pass.

In these circumstances they continued to hold out, not only until the Romans had occupied most of the surrounding area, but even after the fall of Jerusalem itself in the summer of 70. The Roman offensive against this remote outpost of revolt was for one reason or another delayed—a fact which no doubt helped raise Eleazar's expectations. But finally, in the year 73, siege was laid to Masadah. (The Roman siege-works at the foot of the mountain are still virtually intact, again confirming Josephus's description.) In the end, the defenders were starved out, and committed collective suicide rather than surrender. The legionaries then surged into the fortress, which they systematically destroyed.

From that day on, the site was desolate, and being so remote from any inhabited area, remained almost completely untouched. Thus we have an invaluable dateline for anything discovered in the ruins: any findings must necessarily antedate the fifteenth of the month of Xanthicus (i.e., about the beginning of May) in the year 73. Leaving out of the present account the other recent discoveries at this site, let us concentrate on what concerns us most here. Near the ruins of what was apparently a hall that served as a synagogue, Professor Yadin found fragments of various scrolls, mostly Biblical, in a script resembling that of the Dead Sea Scrolls and obviously (if only on paleographical grounds) belonging to the same milieu. Among them is part of a curious liturgical document containing hymns to be sung week by week to correspond with the Sabbath sacrifice—of which other substantial fragments had been found some time before in the Qumran caves! Moreover, this curious liturgy is conceived in accordance with the peculiar, as it were "heretical," calendar of the Qumran sect about which there has been so much discussion among scholars during the past few years.

Thus we now know for certain that the literature and theology of the Dead Sea sect were current at Masadah also: i.e., that the denizens of Masadah belonged to the same body as the sectarians of Qumran, just as I demonstrated in 1957–8. It must be emphasized that the document in question is not of the "'casual" Qumran type—such as a book of praise or psalms, for example, which might have validity anywhere. It is a document of the most clear-cut nature, embodying the most distinctive, and from the point of view of universal Judaism most objectionable, feature of the Qumran sect—their adherence to a unique calendar of their own on the basis of which they calculated their own proper times for the observance of the feasts and even of the Day of Atonement, which times alone were pleasing (and in the last-named case, truly efficacious) in the sight of God. If this literature was current in Masadah, and was read (as seems clear) in the liturgy there, there can be no doubt whatsoever that the defenders of Masadah and the monks of Qumran belonged to the same religious faction. Hence the Qumran sect were neither the ascetic Essenes, nor the aristocratic Sadducees, nor the studious Pharisees, but beyond any doubt the aggressive, bellicose, *Sicarii*-Zealots, dedicated to the doctrine of the sole sovereignty of God over his people.

Professor Yadin, who is responsible for this discovery, but has been from the beginning a stalwart champion of the Essene thesis, has attempted to discount its significance.[1] He explains

[1] Yadin's present arguments against my thesis are already dealt with implicitly in my book and below in Appendix H, which presents, as it seems to me, unanswerable arguments. The expert paleographical dating on which he now leans so heavily is, of course, wholly hypothetical, being based on conjectural foundations: hence it may now be stated conclusively that the Habakkuk commentary was written about the year 70. This is made certain by the references to the 'year of the Four Emperors' and to the worship of the Roman standards in the Temple courtyard: see below.

the presence at Masadah of this remarkable document by the possibility that an Essene fugitive brought it there after the fall of Qumran, the Essenes having by then given up their pacifist principles.[1] But we have no evidence that this was so, or that Essene refugees ever found their way to Masadah—where, with their pacifist record, they could hardly have been welcomed. Were Professor Yadin's thesis admitted, we would have to assume that there existed in Masadah itself at the beginning of the year 73 two different sects, each of which venerated a Teacher of Righteousness who was assailed in Jerusalem by a Wicked Priest on or about the Day of Atonement, and that both Teachers had a close associate named Absalom. Each sect, moreover, would have maintained in the fortress of Masadah its own synagogue in which different liturgies were followed, according to different calendars, so that even the Day of Atonement would have been observed on different dates!

The conclusion is inescapable. The two sects were one, and Qumran was part of the republic of the *Sicarii*-Zealots of Masadah.

Now that the Qumran sect is finally identified with the *Sicarii*-Zealots of Masadah, it is irrefutably established that the literature of the Dead Sea Scrolls is in fact the literature, not of a pre-Christian mystery sect nor of medieval Karaites nor of contemplative Essenes, but rather of the extremist leaders in the great revolt against Rome in 66–73. We were already informed by Josephus how in the last days of the siege the streets of Jerusalem were filled with prophets and prophesies. Now we know something of the nature of those prophesies. We know the language in which they were conceived, as well as something

---

[1] Much attention is hence being paid after nearly two thousand years to the record of the ill-starred insurgent general mentioned by Josephus, John the Essene. Except for his name, we know nothing whatsoever about John except that he was appointed a provincial governor at the outset of the Revolt in the autumn of 66, and fell in the disastrous attack on Ascalon almost immediately afterward. Obviously, therefore, he must have made his name known as a partisan leader either before the Revolt started, or else in the course of the initial operations. Just as obviously, the fact of his existence cannot be used to prove that later on, when the country was in danger, the Essenes as a body (or in large numbers at least) gave up their pacifist principles and took up arms. John may, in fact, never even have been a member of the sect: the designation "Essene" in his case may also mean "the taciturn."

of the ideas and ideals behind them. And we know what incited these grim fighters for freedom to continue the struggle when their whole world had toppled into ruins around them.

What we knew formerly of all this came from the partisan reports of the contemptible Jewish quisling, Flavius Josephus. Now at last we have a glimpse of the spiritual background of the period as it appeared to those whom he betrayed when they were living and vilified when they were dead. I am, I suppose, a bit of a jingoist, but I can hardly imagine a discovery which from the Jewish point of view is more exciting than this final identification of the literature of the last defenders of Jerusalem and Masadah.

THE DEAD SEA SCROLLS

A New Historical Approach

I

Only obstinacy or prejudice can now persist in the view that
the so-called Dead Sea Scrolls, which have engaged the attention of the world of scholarship so persistently during the past
ten years, are no more than 'mediaeval forgeries'. Literary, scientific and archaeological evidences make it certain that in the main
they are not later than the third quarter of the first century A.D.,
when the site in which they were found was abandoned, and which
is the medial date to which the carbon-14 test points. Nor is it
seriously proposed by any scholar that any of the complete texts
antedate the second century B.C., although some Biblical fragments
may well be older.[1] We must therefore place the documents within
these broad chronological limits—that is, between 200 B.C. (or
somewhat later) and A.D. 100 (or, more precisely, a quarter of
a century before). In connection with this enquiry, we must
inevitably concentrate attention on the remarkable (and
fortunately relatively well-preserved) commentary on the Book
of Habakkuk, which is replete with allusions to the history of
the group that produced this literature: obvious enough no doubt
in the circles for which it was intended, but the subject of violent
controversy among scholars ever since the text became known
ten years ago.

Palaeographical evidence is inconclusive, because we have no

---

[1] Bibliographical references will not be needlessly accumulated in this
monograph, as it would take up far too much space to mention or argue against
all those scholars who had expressed or accepted different views. The present
thesis must stand or fall on its own merits.

The total number of publications on the subject, during the past ten years,
is said to exceed 3,000. The most reliable summary in English is that by H. H.
Rowley, *The Zadokite Fragments and the Dead Sea Scrolls* (1955), with very full
bibliography and references which it is pointless to duplicate. There are some
additional data in the same writer's *Jewish Apocalyptic and the Dead Sea Scrolls*
(1957). There are comprehensive works of a more popular type, all however
important for the study of the subject, by Millar Burrows, J. M. Allegro,
Y. Yadin, G. Vermès, A. Dupont-Sommer, &c.

Hebrew script of assured date with which to make any comparison. It is of course legitimate to group these manuscripts in chronological sequence. But to say of any one of them dogmatically (as has come to be done) that it belongs to 'the early part of the first', or 'the middle of the second' century B.C. is premature in our present state of knowledge—and must remain so until we are in a position to apply a definite date, within a few years, to one at least of these newly-found documents. On the other hand, the archaeological evidences (provided that we discard the likelihood of later intrusions) can provide only a *terminus ad quem*, the Qumran 'monastery' where this literature was produced having been destroyed and abandoned about the time of the great Revolt against Rome in A.D. 66–70: but the *terminus a quo* is left open. It is obvious that the assured dating of the commentary on Habakkuk would serve as a hinge whereby the history of the Qumran sect could be swung into historical perspective. Moreover, if it could be demonstrated that the text preserved is more or less contemporary with its composition, we would at last have a fixed point for putting the palaeography of these newly-found documents in a definite chronological setting. The approach to the problem in the present monograph is purely historical: but it will be seen that the purely historical approach, without theological or sentimental bias, provides for the first time not a working theory, but what appears to the author to be an incontrovertible solution.

A cursory reading of the Habakkuk Commentary is enough to show that the writer has in view a period in which Palestine was being relentlessly overrun and its inhabitants imminently threatened by a heathen enemy from across the seas, well-organised and of overwhelming military might, invariably termed here and in the parallel documents the 'Kittim'. Most scholars agree that these are the Romans: no other people of classical antiquity who were in close relations with the Jews conforms even broadly with the picture which these documents convey.[1] That the name was interpreted as 'Romans' in the oldest

---

[1] Refer to Appendix D, which provides new and (as the author feels) irrefutable evidence. The few scholars who still maintain that the Kittim are the Greeks are compelled to do so by their early dating of the historical background of the Scrolls. The recently-discovered gloss on Nahum ii. 12 (published by J. M. Allegro in the Journal of Biblical Literature (=J.B.L.) lxxv, 90, makes it quite certain that the Kittim followed the Greeks.

Jewish translations of the Bible into Aramaic is a fact which cannot be disregarded in this connection, though it should not be over-stressed.[1] Moreover, the menace of the Kittim is depicted as imminent; they are not merely looming in the background, as the Romans were from the beginning of the second century B.C. down to Pompey's invasion of Syria and occupation of Judaea in 65–62 B.C., but they were sweeping or about to sweep through the country, treating its inhabitants as enemies and with the utmost cruelty.

The second aspect of contemporary conditions which pervades these documents is the existence of an unworthy priesthood, in particular one designated as 'the Wicked Priest', who not only controlled the Temple in Jerusalem, but also had great political authority: this he exercised tyrannically, persecuting or even being responsible for the death of the venerated Master of the group which produced this literature ('The Teacher of Righteousness').[2]

We have to find therefore in Jewish history, of the period between 65 B.C. and A.D. 70, circumstances in which

(i)   the menace to Jewish Palestine from the Romans was appallingly acute, although they were not actually in control of the entire country;

(ii) political authority was in the hands of the priesthood, or of priests, so that they were able to persecute or bring about the death of a religious leader who opposed them.[3]

There was in fact only one period of Jewish history when these circumstances prevailed, and at this period such an episode,

---

[1] *E.g.* in the Targum Onkelos to Numbers xxiv, 24.

[2] An entire work has already been devoted to a survey of the numerous attempted identifications of this personage: A. Michel, *Le Maître de Justice d'apres les documents de la Mer Morte*, Avignon 1954.

[3] The fashionable (and sensational) identification with Alexander Jannaeus or some other Hasmonaean ruler of the second century B.C. does not seem to have any validity, for the simple reason that it would not have entered any person's head at that time to refer to these sovereigns as 'priests', without any further description. Since the Rabbis and the Jewish people as a whole violently objected to the concentration in their hands of both civil and sacerdotal power, it would be astonishing that this fact should not be alluded to, however remotely, in these writings. Prof. Dupont-Sommer's persistent attempt to identify the Wicked Priest with King Hyrcanus II (63–40 B.C.) presents that unfortunate and much-suffering ruler, moreover, in a light uncorroborated by any historical source or verisimilitude.

sufficiently familiar, did take place. It was at the beginning of the great Revolt against Rome in A.D. 66–70, which was to be the prelude to the destruction of Jerusalem. But, to understand the circumstances, it is necessary to consider, and to evaluate, the historical sources on which we have to rely for our knowledge.

II

Virtually our only evidence for the history of the Jews at the close of the period of the Second Temple is in the writings of Josephus. That talented historian though by no means admirable character is generally reliable enough as regards facts, so far as we can tell in the absence of any alternative authority. But his interpretations and judgements were always singularly subjective. His views on contemporary events and happenings were consistently guided by one fundamental principle: that whatever he did was right, and that, therefore, whatever his enemies did was *ipso facto* wrong. He was not quite so consistent in his attitude towards the Romans, but the actions of Vespasian and Titus at least were for him always above criticism, their opponents being therefore considered malefactors or maniacs. It is on the basis of these fundamental principles that Josephus presents the heroic story of the great Jewish patriotic rising against Rome, in the early stages of which he took part and which he ultimately betrayed. He speaks of the leaders of the resistance *à outrance* as brigands and assassins, and depicts their internecine quarrels as the outcome of personal ambition or suicidal folly. The tale as he tells it has unfortunately entered into general historiography. But already a century ago Dean Milman realised that there must necessarily have been another side to the story. The fighters for Jewish freedom in beleaguered Jerusalem, as he pointed out, comprised patriots as pure and as devoted as those who have been associated with similar movements throughout history, and those who defended the Temple against the Romans in A.D. 70 were not inferior in nobility to those who defended it against the Babylonians in 586 B.C.

Reading Josephus' pages with this in our minds, we see how the events preceding the fall of Jerusalem, which he presents in so disparaging a fashion, were in the nature not only of a Revolt

but also of a Revolution, of the classical type—beginning with
a Reformist movement, developing into a national uprising, and
ultimately becoming a social revolution which moved constantly
towards greater and greater extremity, and was accompanied by
greater and greater violence. Josephus' 'brigands' and 'assassins'
thus appear as being in fact patriotic (however misguided) revolutionaries, whose great sin was that they opposed at first the Romans,
who were to be his patrons, and then the dominating priesthood
and bourgeoisie, who were his associates. All of this deserves
more careful and thorough exposition.[1] What is desired here is
only to emphasise the fact that, though we have little beyond the
evidence of Josephus to guide us for the events and personalities
of this period,[2] the interpretation of those events and the evaluation
of those personalities must be made quite independently of his
judgements.

In the nature of things, the various parties at the time of the
Revolt could not have been divided only by differences regarding
external, or even of social, policy: for we are dealing, it must be
remembered, with the first century, when Judaea was in a perpetual fever of religious excitement. At such a time these divergences must necessarily have had to some extent a religious
impulse. The revolutionaries were convinced that God was on
their side, and that in their strivings they were fulfilling the will
of God. This indeed made it all the more difficult for them to
compromise with their internal opponents, however serious the
military situation. For obviously, it was only when the will of God
was being fulfilled in every detail, in the matter of ceremonial
observance as well as of social justice, that He would vouchsafe
His people victory. Except, perhaps, as regards that doughty
patriotic fighter John of Gischala, their concern was not merely
to triumph over the Romans, but also, as a preliminary or a
concomitant, to establish the Kingdom of Heaven on earth—for
then assuredly God would manifest Himself in all His glory and
rout their enemies. Once we understand this, all the internecine
strife falls into shape and makes sense. Only after Error was
suppressed among the Jewish people and Virtue was supreme,

---

[1] The present writer hopes to publish shortly a presentation of the 'Jewish
Revolution' in this light.

[2] Especially his *Wars of the Jews* (to be referred to as *Wars*) and to a minor
extent his *Antiquities* (=*Ant.*). Use will be made as far as possible of the (unfinished) Loeb Classics version.

could they hope for Divine succour—even at the last hour, when human succour was beyond expectation. We now understand how even the suicidal action of burning the granaries had its own wild apocalyptic logic, for by bringing the city more rapidly to the last extremity it hastened the moment when God would manifest Himself to save His people.

This digression has been essential for our purpose. For it is necessary to realise that some at least of those whom Josephus depicts as demented cut-throats, and modern nationalist Jewish historians (such as Joseph Klausner) as patriotic heroes, must necessarily have been at the same time social reformers and religious teachers, all record of whose doctrine perished (or so it formerly appeared) in the subsequent disaster.

It is fundamental to an understanding of the history of this period to realise that our modern ideas of the division of the military, the political, the religious, and the ceremonial spheres now have no validity. The political leader at the same time commanded the forces in the field, tried to achieve a religious revival, worked for moral reform, preached social justice, and meanwhile insisted on a more meticulous observance of the ceremonial observances according to his personal interpretation. When man dealt towards man with perfect justice, when the ritual precepts of the Law were punctually carried out in the minutest detail, when the Sabbath was properly observed, then and then only could the people triumph over their enemies: and to do all these things was indeed the way whereby triumph would be ensured. With all this in mind, let us turn back to the pages of Josephus.

III

In the present connection, attention will be concentrated on one single character, who makes in the historian's pages a tantalisingly brief but most unfavourable appearance: Menahem, son of Judah the Galilaean. His grandfather was apparently the patriotic partisan leader Hezekiah 'a brigand chief at the head of a large horde' who was hunted down and summarily put to death on the Syrian frontier by Herod at the outset of his career, about 47 B.C. The latter's son was Judah (Judas), who after Herod's death rose in revolt in Galilee. He is presumably identical with

Judah 'the Galilaean', of Gamala in Gaulanitis, who about
A.D. 6 founded the sect or party of the Zealots. From then onwards
the latter were in a state of perpetual revolt: their fundamental
religious principle being that it was wrong to pay tribute to the
Romans or to tolerate mortal masters, after having God for their
Lord. In due course, Judah was killed, but the patriotic sect
which he founded maintained itself in being, members of his
family always remaining at its head. It seems indeed as though
the sect attached great importance to the hereditary principle;
possibly, the family had specific Messianic pretensions. Two of
Judah's sons, Jacob and Simon, were captured in the field by
Tiberius Alexander, the apostate procurator of Judaea in A.D.
46–48, probably in the course of an uprising, and were cruelly
put to death. The leadership now devolved on their brother,
Menahem, who by the time of the Revolt against Rome must
have been well on in years.[1]

Josephus calls him, as well as his father, a 'sophist' (Judah is
'an outstanding sophist'[2]). It is a title which he applies elsewhere
to persons learned in the Jewish law, perhaps Rabbis. We cannot
define its application exactly, but obviously it implies that the
person so styled was an intellectual and a teacher, holding (one
may presume) theories and views on religion and life which he
endeavoured to transmit to his disciples.[3] This is very important:

[1] There are slight but superable chronological difficulties involved in this
genealogical scheme, stated all but categorically by Josephus. It should however be borne in mind that all the successive leaders met with violent deaths
under arms, Hezekiah and Judah being presumably still young. The former
could have been born in 77 B.C. and died as we know in 47 B.C.; his son could
have been born about 50 B.C., and was a child at the time of his father's violent
death, himself dying in A.D. 6; Menahem, a younger son of Judah's, might
have been born therefore at the beginning of the Christian era, and have
been in the middle sixties at the time of the Revolt against Rome. It will not
however affect the thesis here presented if the name of Hezekiah is left out of
consideration.

[2] The text of *Wars*, II, xvii, 8, §433 is confused; it is therefore doubtful
whether the phrase σοφιστὴς δεινότατος refers to Menahem or to Judah, and
indeed whether it occurred at all in the original form.

[3] The term is applied by the second-century Greek satirist Lucian (*De morte
peregrini*, §13) to Jesus, as I am informed by Prof. G. R. Driver. Josephus
applies it (in the plural) in *Wars*, I, xxiii, 2 §648–9 (cf. *Ant.* XVII, vi, 2 §15)
to the two hyper-patriotic scholars who were martyred by Herod for leading
the protest against the erection of the golden eagle over the gateway of the
Temple. He amplifies the term by adding that they had 'a reputation as profound experts in the laws of their country'.

it shows clearly that Menahem was not merely an ambitious partisan leader, as Josephus tries to depict him.

At the time of the outbreak of the revolt against Rome, in the summer of A.D. 66, Menahem and his followers seized the fortress-palace of Masadah, high above the Dead Sea; here the Zealots remained in complete control for the next eight years, their authority extending also to some surrounding territory. The capture of this stronghold moreover put them in control of the armoury established there by Herod for use in emergency, which Menahem used to equip his followers. Thus he was now able to march on Jerusalem with a devoted and well-provided band of adherents, hardened by years of partisan fighting and encouraged by one signal success. The contingent arrived apparently after open hostilities had broken out in the capital. The fortress of Antonia was about to fall into the hands of the insurgents, the Roman garrison with their native sympathisers being then besieged in the strongly-fortified royal palace in the Upper City. Menahem now assumed command of the assailants, and directed the siege. He seems to have shown some military ability. Before long the bulk of the garrison capitulated, though the Roman troops were to hold out a little longer in the fortified bastions. Some of the leading pro-Romans who had taken refuge in the palace were hunted down and killed by the triumphant patriot forces, one of them being Hananiah (Ananias), a former high-priest.

Josephus describes the succeeding events as in a graphic passage (*Wars*, II, xvii, 9, §§442–8):—

'But the reduction of the strongholds and the murder of the high-priest Ananias inflated and brutalized Menahem to such an extent that he believed himself without a rival in the conduct of affairs and became an insufferable tyrant. The partisans of Eleazar [the priest, Captain of the Temple] now rose against him; they remarked to one another that, after revolting from the Romans for love of liberty, they ought not to sacrifice this liberty to a Jewish hangman and to put up with a master who, even were he to abstain from violence, was anyhow far below themselves; and that if they must have a leader, anyone would be better than Menahem. So they laid their plans to attack him in the Temple, whither he had gone up in state to prostrate himself, royally arrayed and attended by an escort of armed zealots. When Eleazar and his companions rushed upon him, and the rest of the people to gratify their rage took up stones and began pelting the arrogant sophist, imagining that his downfall would crush the whole revolt, Menahem and his followers offered a momentary resistance; then, seeing themselves assailed by the whole multitude, they fled whithersoever they could; all who were caught were massacred, and a hunt was made for any in hiding.... Menahem himself, who had taken refuge in the place called Ophlas and there ignominiously concealed himself, was caught, dragged into the open, and put to death after being subjected to all kinds of torture ...'

Let us try to restate this in objective terms. The revolt in Jerusalem had started as a reformist movement, aimed at removing abuses in administration, and only secondarily against the Romans. The outstanding figure in the early stages was Eleazar, son of Hananiah (Ananias), the Priest, Captain of the Temple, who had induced his colleagues to withhold the daily sacrifice in the name of the Emperor, thus in effect repudiating allegiance to the Romans. His principal associates were other priestly aristocrats who considered indeed that they were the natural rulers of Judaea, as their predecessors had been in normal circumstances ever since the Return from the Babylonian Exile. The list of the insurgent leaders to whom the principal offices of state were subsequently entrusted, among them Josephus himself, confirms this picture of a 'hierocracy'; out of nine persons appointed to the highest office, four at least were priests (*Wars*, II, xx, 3, §§562–5).[1] This reformist, priestly and aristocratic element found themselves pushed out of the way by Menahem and his eager followers, with the prestige of their signal successes in the field and of a long tradition of uncompromising resistance to the Romans. Clearly, Menahem now considered himself, not without reason, to be the leader of the revolt—possibly even the deliverer designated by God—and no doubt wished to impose his personal religious and political programme on the country. The priestly revolutionaries in Jerusalem did not object apparently only to this, but also to his origins and background; for he was, as they said, 'so far below themselves', and possibly also advocated a more egalitarian

[1] See the names of the Revolutionary administration in *Wars*, II, xx, 3 §562 ff: Josephus is not himself described as a Priest, and perhaps the same may be the case with some others, in which event the proportion is even higher. To speak of the revolutionary government at this time as a priestly junta is certainly no exaggeration.

social programme (this aspect of Zealot policy was to become more and more apparent as the Revolution progressed). Moreover, they may have feared not only for their position but also for their lives, when suspected Roman sympathizers were being pitilessly hunted down: Josephus tells us in his autobiography that at this time he sought refuge in the inner court of the Temple, venturing out only when the chieftains of the 'band of brigands' had been put to death.[1]

However that may be, Menahem's enemies, feeling that their position was threatened, now combined against him. It appears from Josephus' account that they inflamed the populace by alleging that he had royal ambitions, and thus managed to stir up feeling against him when he went to the Temple with his followers to perform his devotions.[2] Eleazar, who was more or less in control here, took the opportunity to attack him. A riot ensued, fomented by the priestly party: there were casualties: and Menahem himself was hunted down on the hill of Ophel (the eastern hill, to the south of the Temple) where he had taken refuge. Here he was ferociously done to death by his opponents, together with many of his followers. The survivors, headed by his kinsman (probably a nephew) Eleazar ben Jair, took refuge back in Masadah, which with its environs remained in their hands. Menahem's assassination took place very shortly after the capitulation of the royal palace, which according to Josephus was on the sixth day of the month of Gorpiaeus (August–September).

Now, a central fact in the historic experience of the Qumran Sect was an episode connected with the Teacher of Righteousness which took place on the Day of Atonement. The importance attached to this is seen in the now-famous passage of the Habakkuk Commentary (xi, 3–8), which is the fundamental document for determining the chronological and historical setting of the sect's history. We may render the passage as follows:—

'*Woe unto him that giveth his neighbour drink, that addeth his rage thereto, making him drunken, in order that he may gaze upon their festive seasons* [Hab. ii, 15, with textual variants]: Its interpretation concerns the Wicked Priest, who pursued the Teacher of Righteousness, to swallow him up in the anger of his rage

[1] *Vita*, §21. This passage makes it clear that Menahem had been responsible also for the reduction of the Antonia fortress.

[2] See below, pp. 60-2 for an alternative explanation of this episode.

in the place of his revealing. And at the fixed time of the season of the repose of the Day of Atonement he appeared to them, to swallow them up and to make them stumble, on the fast-day Sabbath of their repose.'

The exact meaning of this passage is very difficult to determine (the English rendering is intentionally made to reflect the obscurity and ambiguities of the original) and we shall have occasion to reconsider it later in detail.[1] We may however deduce, at the least, that there was a clash between the Wicked Priest and the Teacher of Righteousness, on the Day of Atonement, possibly in the Temple.

That this encounter resulted in or was immediately followed by the violent death of the Teacher of Righteousness is not stated in unambiguous terms in the Habakkuk Commentary, though it is possibly implied in the repeated phrase, 'to swallow him [them] up'. For this to imply his assassination would be in accordance with the normal Hebrew idiom, and was assumed from the outset by most scholars, this being the basis of the discussions about the historic setting of the Qumran sect.[2] This interpretation seems to be conveyed not only by the language but also by the general tenor of our documents—which we must remember are by no means complete, and in any case may not have considered it necessary to speak in specific terms of an event so notorious and so fundamental to the sect's history. Moreover, a passage in the (unfortunately fragmentary) commentary on Psalm xxxvii, discovered and published more recently, demonstrates the serious sequel to the encounter on the Day of Atonement:—[3]

'*The wicked watcheth the righteous and seeketh to slay him. The Lord will not leave him in his hand, nor consider him guilty when he is judged* (Ps. xxxvii, 32-3): Its interpretation concerns the Wicked Priest who sent against . . . to kill him . . .[?] and the Law that he sent to him and God will not . . . and pay his recompense, to deliver him in the hand of the Terrible Ones of the Gentiles . . . '

---

[1] See Appendix A on the interpretation of this involved passage.

[2] See Appendix B: 'Was the Teacher of Righteousness put to death?'

[3] Published by Allegro in J.B.L. lxxv, 94. I am informed by Mr. Allegro that another unpublished fragment applies 'He giveth his beloved sleep' (Ps. cxxvii, 2) to the Teacher of Righteousness.

There can be little doubt that this refers to the same episode as the passage in the Habakkuk Commentary, making certain its sanguinary intention or outcome.

Various attempts have been made, as we have seen, to identify the protagonists in this encounter, but always details have been assumed regarding which our sources provide us with no information. On the other hand, the passage applies, precisely, to the circumstances which we have been considering.

The writer, a member of the Qumran group, was in the area of the Dead Sea, the centre of the Zealots, where the adepts of that 'philosophy' were still centred at Masadah under the leadership of Eleazar ben Jair; he was presumably not only their captain in the field, when they carried out armed raids on their opponents, but also their teacher, like the other leaders of the 'sect' before him. Not long previously, his predecessor, Menahem ben Judah, who was known as a sophist (a man that is who had a religious as well as a political programme) and who considered himself to be designated by God to redeem his people, had led his followers to Jerusalem, where he had achieved a striking military success. On the sixth day of the month Gorpiaeus his followers had stormed Herod's palace, forced the garrison to capitulate, and driven the surviving Roman troops into the bastions, where it was obvious that they would be unable to hold out for long. This date has been reckoned as corresponding to 3 Tishri in the Hebrew calendar.[1] Shortly after, we are told by Josephus, Menahem went up to the Temple 'in state', royally arrayed— not only to perform his devotions, but presumably also to preach his doctrine, or perhaps even with the intention to officiate.[2] It is important to note that this must have coincided nearly enough with the Day of Atonement (10 Tishri). But in coming to the Temple, he had placed himself in the hands of his enemies. The triumph was succeeded by disaster. The 'Wicked Priest',

[1] S. Zeitlin, *Megillat Taanit as a Source for Jewish Chronology and History* (Philadelphia, 1922: reprinted from Jewish Quarterly Review, n.s.) pp. 97–9. In any case, it was the period of the autumn solemnities of the Jewish religious year: for reasons that will appear later, the precise correspondence according to the accepted calendar is irrelevant. It is not easy to see why Zeitlin bases his calculation on the reckoning for the year 65, not the universally-accepted 66, but the matter is of minor significance in the present context. In 66, according to the same authority, 6 Gorpiaeus corresponded to 14 Tishri.

[2] See pp. 60–2 below for a development of this point, and also of the calendrical problem.

Eleazar ben Hananiah, Captain of the Temple, who opposed
both the Teacher's political claims and his religious doctrines,
raised an artificial riot against him, and almost immediately
afterwards he was done to death. The parallel with the story of
the Teacher of Righteousness is too close to be accidental.

A further coincidence seems to clinch this identification beyond
any possibility of doubt. The Habakkuk Commentary, in another
passage (v. 8–12) glosses:—

> '*Wherefore do you look on, ye treacherous, and keep thy silence, when
> the wicked one swalloweth up one more righteous than himself*: Its
> interpretation concerns the House of Absalom and the men
> of their counsel, who were silent at the time of the suffering
> of the Teacher of Righteousness, and did not help him against
> the Man of Lies, who rejected the Law in the midst of all their
> congregation.'[1]

A current opinion is that the 'House of Absalom' here refers
to the wayward in general, with a vague reminiscence of the
Biblical account of the unfilial revolt of David's son of that name.
Another view suggests the name of Absalom, uncle and father-
in-law of the Hasmonaean sovereign Aristobulus II, with whose
name the episode of the Teacher of Righteousness has been
associated. But there is no need to resort to hypothesis: we have
a positive reference to a second sectarian leader of the name of
Absalom, in connection with the episode to which attention has
been directed above. At the end of his story of the assassination
of Menahem, Josephus goes on to say: 'His lieutenants, along
with Absalom, his most noteworthy assistant in his tyranny, met
with a similar fate'. It seems that Josephus differentiates between
Menahem's lieutenants and Absalom, his assistant (ὑπηρέτης)
—that is to say, apparently an independent leader, close to but not
identical with Menahem in his outlook. Absalom then was perhaps

[1] Refer to Appendix C ('The House of Absalom'), for a detailed
discussion of this difficult passage. All that can be definitely deduced is that
they were concerned with the crisis of the Teacher of Righteousness, should
have supported him, but proved unreliable. Most names in this literature are
used typologically. But the name Absalom does not immediately suggest any
specific type, much less the House of Absalom: obviously only major figures
could be alluded to in this manner with some prospect of recognition.
As a matter of fact, notwithstanding what has been said on the subject,
no *contemporary* is referred to in the Scrolls by a typological name, though
many are by permanent epithets.

at the head of a subdivision of the Zealot party, with their own views on certain matters. In any case, his followers did not support Menahem, when he came into conflict with the Man of Lies (who may or may not be identical with the Wicked Priest). Nevertheless, in the eyes of the outside world they were closely associated, notwithstanding doctrinal divergences: for when Eleazar attacked Menahem he did not spare Absalom, 'his most eminent supporter in his tyranny' who also perished in the disorders. Whatever the exact interpretation, which is not easy to determine, it is obvious that Absalom was a person who should have supported the Teacher, but whose followers at some critical moment did not do so.[1] The mention here of the 'House' of Absalom suggests that their leader was no longer on the scene, having already been a victim of the disturbances.[2]

This seems to place beyond reasonable question the identification of the 'sophist' Menahem (or his successor, who shared his experience but survived) with the Teacher of Righteousness. It remains however to see

    (i) whether there is any evidence that Menahem's memory was reverenced after his death, and

    (ii) what connection his followers can have had with Qumran.

IV

Josephus gives adequate information for determining the history of the stronghold of Masadah, on the west coast of the Dead Sea, from the beginning of the reign of Herod onwards. He tells in detail how that monarch constructed there his almost impregnable palace, relics of which, strikingly confirming the historian's account, have recently been discovered and investi-

---

[1] The episode is discussed more extensively in Appendix C. Against my identification of Absalom it has been argued (*cf.* P. Winter in the *Manchester Guardian*, June 1, 1957; Dupont-Sommer in *Evidences*, December 1957) that according to Josephus he was a supporter, not opponent, of Menahem. This illustrates the dangers of attempting to solve historical problems without historical perspective: it is surely self-evident that indifference at a time of crisis is cause for blaming allies, not enemies.

[2] For evidence that Ophel, where Menahem met his fate, may have figured specifically in the Qumran literature as the scene of the culminating experience of the Teacher of Righteousness, see Appendix F.

gated. In the summer of A.D. 66, at the beginning of the anti-Roman disorders in Jerusalem, some of the most ardent promoters of hostilities banded themselves together and made an assault on the fortress; having gained possession of it by a stratagem, they slew the Roman guards and put a garrison of their own in their place (*Wars*, II, xvii, 2, §408). This account is supplemented later (*Ibid.* 8, §§433–4) when Josephus characteristically informs us that the patriot leader responsible for this was Menahem ben Judah who 'took his associates with him to Masadah, where he broke into king Herod's armoury and provided arms both for his accomplices and for other brigands.' (Whether this was a second raid, displacing the original partisan force, or whether we now have a slightly ampler account of the same episode is not quite clear, but the latter is more probable.) It was this success which gave Menahem the confidence and equipment to march to Jerusalem, where his arrival with his well-armed followers turned the tide of battle, as we have seen. After his overthrow his surviving followers escaped back to Masadah, under the leadership of his kinsman Eleazar ben Jair, who remained in control of the stronghold for some seven or eight years, until A.D. 73, and was then to figure as the last desperate hero of Jewish independence.

From a careful reading of Josephus' account, several points of great importance for our present investigation emerge. In the first place, it is obvious that the Zealots in Masadah did not consider that they owed allegiance to the Jewish revolutionary authorities in Jerusalem: clearly, there were ideological factors which made this impossible, even when the priestly faction responsible for Menahem's death had been swept aside. For these Zealots, like others in the same position at all times, were convinced of their own rectitude, and would not compromise with those who did not think as they did. At one time, Simon bar Giora, the extreme revolutionary and egalitarian, who to the dismay of the conservatives went so far as to free the slaves, joined the Masadah group, but in due course they parted company. Obviously therefore there must have been basic differences between them: they perhaps could not accept his social programme, he could not accept their religious outlook. Moreover, even when Jerusalem was besieged by the Roman legions and reduced to its last extremity, Eleazar and his followers did not march to help in its defence, nor so far as we know did they attempt any serious and concerted diversionary activity. It is certain therefore that there must have been a profound gulf between the two parties. Eleazar ben Jair disapproved what was going on in Jerusalem, and could not believe that God would give the defenders victory in such circumstances.[1] In this, he differed perhaps from another wing of the Zealots, who remained in the city under Eleazar ben Simon; long maintained themselves in the Temple area and thereby were able to control the sacrificial service; tried to master the other factions; and when they were worsted continued to fight to the end, under the more secular John of Gischala.[2]

The Zealot occupation of Masadah lasted, as stated, for about six or seven years: there must have been therefore some sort of settled administration, even though the spirit may have been akin to that of a revivalist camp. Moreover, it was not a passive but an active and expanding society, in theory at least. Josephus tells us (*Wars*, IV, vii, 2, §§399–404) of the Zealot raids from this centre on neighbouring districts. What was more important for our purpose: apparently in the spring of A.D. 68, they captured from the Jewish forces the town of Engedi, also on the Dead Sea coast, to the north of their stronghold. Josephus states, with his habitual somewhat unreal horror (*Ibid*. 2, §402), that this took place on the feast of Passover. The Zealots however were *ex hypothesi* highly orthodox in practice. One may therefore suggest the possibility that the garrison at Masadah had a different reckoning of time so that they did not consider this to be a feast-day. This would strengthen the identification with the Qumran 'sect', whose use of a different calendar is as we shall see definitely established. In the same area, Machaerus, Herodium, and an unidentified place 'the forest called Jardes', also long held out against the Romans: although we are not specifically informed that their garrisons were Zealot, this may well have been the case. Josephus asserts (*Wars*, VII, vi, 4, §191) that, when the Romans besieged Machaerus, the defenders treated the other inhabitants as foreigners, abandoning them to their fate: this

[1] That the Masadah (Dead Sea) Zealot centre was fiercely opposed to the other revolutionaries is clear from *Wars*, IV, ix, 5, §§514–520. There are obvious historic parallels to this two-headed revolt against an occupying power: *e.g.* in Italy in 1942–5, when the monarchist and communist partisans wrangled with one another in the intervals of fighting the Germans.

[2] A significant piece of evidence confirming the hypothesis that the Qumran sectaries were connected with the Zealot party was the selection of the High Priest by lot after the revolt against the Romans: see below, p. 39.

seems to imply that the former thought of themselves as a separate group. From all this, it appears that the Zealots not only maintained an orderly administration in Masadah for several years but also extended their authority over a fairly considerable area to the north, along the coast of the Dead Sea, *including the area of Qumran.*[1] Here too therefore, as well as in Masadah, the name of their former leader Menahem ben Judah was revered and his teachings perpetuated by his erstwhile pupils and followers, for some while after his death.[2]

We now have therefore the connection between the group in Masadah, venerating the memory of a sophist-teacher with an associate named Absalom, who was killed by a priest of Jerusalem about the time of the Day of Atonement; and the neighbouring group in Qumran, venerating the memory of a teacher with an associate named Absalom, who was killed[3] by a priest of Jeru-

[1] But Qumran may have been (and probably was) occupied by the Zealots before Masadah, as will be seen later.

[2] There is evidence that Menahem's memory was sympathetically remembered long afterwards in Rabbinic circles—unlike that of most of the others associated with the revolt. A Talmudic statement (jBer. II, v: see L. Ginzberg's comment *ad. loc.*: bSan. f. 98b: Midrash Rabba, Lamentations i, 57, basing itself on Lam. i, 16) curiously asserts that the name of the Messiah will be Menahem ben Hezekiah (for the intermediate name, Judah, to be omitted is not unparalleled). No great importance should be attached to this, but it is noteworthy that there are similar apparent allusions to other members of the dynasty. Judah the Galilaean for example seems to be recorded in connection with an argument regarding the impropriety of including the name of the Emperor in documents mentioning God (M. Yadaim, iv, 8). It may be germane to call attention to the half-legendary scholar Menahem who was formerly associated with Hillel (M. Hagigah i̇, 2), 'went forth' to the service of the King (*sc.* God?) accompanied by eighty pairs of disciples all equipped in silk (סיריקון: but cf. סיקרין = *sicarii*: b Hag. 16b), whose countenances later became darkened like pots. They thereby separated themselves from the body of the Jewish people (j Hag. II, ii). All this taken in conjunction seems to preserve in a very garbled form the record of a former Pharisaic leader and teacher at the beginning of the Christian era who became an heresiarch: possibly however merging in this is the recollection of the saintly Essene Menahem recorded by Josephus who became a favourite of Herod (*Ant.* XV, x, 5, §§ 373–8). See Appendix D.

[3] The argument does not lose its validity if the term 'persecuted' is substituted for 'killed', and the name of Eleazar ben Jair, his companion and successor, for that of Menahem: see Appendix B.

It is unnecessary to justify the use of the term 'venerate' to describe the attitude of the Masadah zealots towards Menahem after his death. It would be curious if the memory of the hereditary leader of the sect in the third generation were not venerated after his assassination or death.

salem about[1] the time of the Day of Atonement. Qumran was in the political orbit of Masadah, and continued to be for some years, so that we might almost speak of the Republic of Masadah-Qumran: and the sophist-teacher of Masadah is necessarily identical with the Teacher of Righteousness of Qumran. Or let us put it in another way. It is believed that the 'monastery' at Qumran was occupied and its sect continued to exist until at least A.D. 68. If then the identification suggested here is not accepted, we would have to assume that in the years A.D. 66–8, if not longer (for in fact the time-limit is somewhat more extended than this, as we shall see) there were at Qumran and at Masadah two different groups venerating the memory of two sophist-teachers, each of them with an associate of the name of Absalom, and each assailed by a 'wicked' priest of Jerusalem about the time of the Day of Atonement. A coincidence so preposterously extended and duplicated is out of the question. The Teacher of Righteousness then was necessarily Menahem ben Judah, the Zealot leader, who was done to death by Eleazar ben Hananiah the Priest, Captain of the Temple, in the early autumn of A.D. 66; or the nephew who shared his experience but escaped.[2]

We shall see later that this hypothesis will help us in great measure to reconstruct the history of this period and to identify other events and persons mentioned in the Dead Sea scrolls. Only one point need concern us at the present stage. In retribution for the sufferings of the Teacher of Righteousness, according to the writer of the Habakkuk Commentary in two passages

[1] 'About', not 'on', since a bitter dispute raged as we shall see regarding the proper date of the solemnity.

[2] The reference in the Habakkuk Commentary (viii, 8–9) to the fact that the Wicked Priest was 'called in the name of truth at the commencement of his standing' strengthens the identification with Eleazar, who as has been mentioned was responsible for the repudiation of allegiance to Rome, thereby no doubt temporarily earning Zealot approval. Possibly he based his action specifically on their fundamental doctrine, that the Jews might acknowledge no earthly sovereign.

Josephus (*Ant.*, XX, ix, 3, §§208–10) records that under the procurator Albinus (A.D. 62–4) Eleazar's secretary was seized by the Sicarii as a hostage for one of their number who had been taken prisoner: Eleazar (or his father: the text is corrupt) thereupon persuaded the Procurator to release them. It was long since suggested (A.H.M. Jones, *The Herods of Judaea*, p. 230) that this was the result of collusion. Perhaps this episode might have been interpreted as 'being called in the name of truth at the commencement of his standing'.

(viii, 13–ix, 2; ix, 8–13), the Wicked Priest was himself punished by a violent death, preceded by judicial torture:—

> '*Shall they not rise up suddenly that shall bite thee* etc. Its interpretation concerns the Priest who rebelled and transgressed the commands of God. . . . They were tortured by the judgements of wickedness and the horrors of evil sicknesses they wrought in him and revenges in the body of his flesh'.
>
> '*Because of (the) man's blood, and for the violence done to the Land, to the city and all who dwell therein.* Its interpretation concerns the Wicked Priest who, for the sin against the Teacher of Righteousness and the men of his Counsel, God gave him into the hands of his enemies to afflict him with a plaguing and to consume him with bitterness of the soul, because he did wickedly with God's chosen one'.

These passages confirm what may be deduced from Josephus regarding the subsequent fate of Eleazar, Captain of the Temple. After the assassination of Menahem, he resumed or assumed command of the Jewish insurgent forces in Jerusalem, and received the capitulation of the Roman garrison besieged in the bastions: according to the historian (*Wars*, II, xx, 4, §456) he was mainly responsible for their subsequent massacre.[1] Subsequently, he was sent to Idumaea as one of the two generals

---

[1] It is conceivable that there is a reference to this too in the Habakkuk scroll. The Qumran sect were strict Sabbatarians, their regulations in this respect being more vigorous than those of Pharisaic Judaism: the Book of Jubilees (1: 12–13), which figured among their literature and apparently emanated from the same environment, regards warfare on the day of rest as a capital offence. According to a very plausible reconstruction of a defective passage of the Commentary, there was a particularly heinous instance of the breach of the Sabbath at the time of the clash between the Priest and the Teacher of Righteousness:—

'*Therefore is the law slacked* &c. (Hab. i, 4–5). Its interpretation . . . and the sinners with the Man of Lies, because they did not (obey the instructions?) of the Teacher of Righteousness from the mouth of God . . . for they did not believe the Covenant of God and did not observe His holy Sabbath'.

This seems to refer to a specific occasion. Now, Josephus informs us (*Wars*, II, xvii, 10 §449 ff.) how the Roman garrison of Jerusalem was butchered by the Captain of the Temple and his forces, adding (§456): 'For, to add to its heinousness, the massacre took place on the sabbath, a day on which from religious scruples Jews abstain even from the most innocent acts'. The implication stands even if the phrase 'man of falsehood' applies as suggested elsewhere to some other partisan leader of the time (e.g. to Simon bar Giora: see below, p. 43). This was clearly an act of offensive warfare, forbidden even after defensive warfare was permitted at the outset of the Hasmonaean revolt.

appointed to the southern command. The patronymic is given
in the Greek text on this occasion as 'Neus', but there does not
seem to be much doubt that the Captain of the Temple is in
question, as is normally assumed; his associate being Jesus son
of Sapphas, also 'one of the chief priests'. This is the last that we
hear of either of them. There is however every reason to believe
that after the débâcle in Galilee they, with the rest of their
colleagues (*e.g.* the patriot leader Niger, formerly Governor
of Idumaea) were 'liquidated', to use the modern phrase
(*Wars*, II, xix, 2, §520 and xx, 4, §566; IV, vi, 1, §§359–365) as
the Revolution took a more radical turn and the reign of terror
began in the capital.[1] Josephus describes in some detail how the
extremists (*Wars*, IV, v, 4, §334 ff) now set up a Revolutionary
Tribunal ('Having now come to loathe indiscriminate massacre,
they instituted mock trials and courts of justice'), from which
few of those accused could escape; those in prison even before
this being 'scourged and racked, and only when their bodies
could no longer sustain these tortures were they grudgingly
consigned to the sword' (*Ibid.* 3, §329). The, correspondence
with the picture given in the Habakkuk commentary, of judicial
torture ('torture by the judgements of wickedness . . . and revenge
in the body of his flesh') followed apparently by sickness and in
the end by execution, is exact. The Commentary thus corroborates
and completes the information given by Josephus in a wholly
plausible and persuasive fashion.[2]

[1] The arguments here put forward are unaffected if the Wicked Priest is
identified not with Eleazar the Captain of the Temple but with some other
Priestly leader—*e.g.* his father, the 'chief Priest Ananias' (not necessarily identical with the pro-Roman High Priest of that name killed by Menahem's
Zealot followers in Jerusalem after the capture of the palace?) or Hanan
(Ananus) ben Hanan, High Priest for three months in 62 (when he was responsible for the trial of James, brother of Jesus: *Ant.* XX, ix, 1, §200). The
latter according to Josephus (*Wars*, II, xx, 3, §563; xxii, 1, §647, 651) was
together with Joseph ben Gorion the leading figure in the governing junta in
the Capital in the second stage of the Revolution, after Eleazar ben Hananiah
had receded into obscurity, and later was to be the most eminent victim of
the Reign of Terror (*Wars*, IV, v, 2, §§314–8). The *pešer* on Psalm xxxvii
(below, p. 38) suggests that the Priest was the victim of the Gentiles (עריצי
גואים) but the text is very defective and the reconstruction dubious. Possibly
he survived, to be sentenced by the Romans when Jerusalem fell.

[2] Another detail we are told about the Wicked Priest is that he was responsible for 'the violence done to the Land', this referring to 'the cities of
Judah wherein he stole the property of the poor' (Hab. Commentary xii,
7–10). This falls into relation with what Josephus tells us (*Ant.* XX, ix, 2

The identity of the Teacher of Righteousness on the one hand, and that of the Wicked Priest on the other, thus seem to be definitely established.[1] The Habakkuk Commentary, which was obviously composed very shortly after the events to which it refers, must therefore belong to the period between A.D. 66 and 68 (or perhaps, for reasons which will later emerge, a year or so after), as the deposit in which the document was found is believed to have been closed at this time. Not only this, but the copy in our hands must belong to the same half-decade. Moreover, the related documents originated in the same milieu, and presumably in approximately the same period. We thus for the first time obtain a certain date, within a margin of a very few years, for one of the manuscripts from Qumran: on the strength of this, it should prove possible to submit the others to a more objective and scientific examination from the palaeographical point of view than has hitherto been possible. Moreover: if the identification of the persons and the circumstances in question is accepted, within the framework of Jewish history at the period of the Fall of Jerusalem, the circumstances and many of the allusions of the Qumran literature as a whole now fall into place, with a remarkable and indeed almost uncanny smoothness.[2]

---

§§206-7) regarding the merciless plundering of the Judaean countryside by the servants of the High Priest Ananias—presumably under the direction of his son, Eleazar, as Captain of the Temple. This is additional evidence for the identification here suggested.

[1] The names of Menahem and Absalom were associated with the Teacher of Righteousness with insufficient demonstration by H. E. Del Medico, *Deux manuscrits hébreux de la mer morte,* Paris 1951, and *L'énigme des manuscrits de la mer morte,* Paris 1957. (He however converts Menahem into a Sadducee, is certain that he was not a son of Judah the Galilaean, and proposes that he was a follower and relative of the High Priest Anan!) The identity of the Qumran sect with the Sicarii has been proposed by Klausner in an appendix to the later editions of his Hebrew *History of the Second Temple.* The present argument does not however turn on a casual coincidence of detail, but on the full identification of the circumstances and background.

[2] While what will be said from now on seems to follow logically from the suggestion put forward in the previous pages of this paper, the two are not necessarily bound up together. That is to say, even if the identity of the Qumran sect with the Zealots, and the consequent reconstruction of their history, should not command assent, the identifications proposed above would not be affected.

V

A corollary of primary importance which follows from the identification of the Teacher of Righteousness with Menahem ben Judah is that *the group which had its centre at Qumran was identical with the Zealots*, the politico-religious body founded by Menahem's father. The Qumran literature thus reflects the history and politico-religious programme of the Zealots. Moreover, the so-called Zadokite Documents having a very close connection with this group (as is now certain, fragments of several copies of this composition having been found in the Qumran caves) these too[1] must have originated in Zealot circles. We thus face an extraordinary new situation: of the four known Jewish sects which flourished at the time of the birth of Christianity, we have now an unrivalled documentation precisely of the one of which we hitherto knew least.

Hitherto, attention has been concentrated on three only of those sects which existed at this time—the Sadducees, Pharisees and Essenes, to which Josephus also adds the semi-political Zealots. If however the occupants of Qumran were none of these, it would be necessary in the light of the recent finds to add yet a fifth sect with a considerable literature of its own, which Josephus did not mention: a point which would itself require explanation. That the group at Qumran were not Sadducees, aristocratic in tendency, rejecting angelology and the future life, and with their attention concentrated on the Temple-ritual, is self-evident. Their monastic life, also in the area of the Dead Sea, gives them obvious analogies with the Essenes, but only analogies: for they were not misogynists, they did not practise community of property, they tolerated slavery, they did not disapprove of animal sacrifice, they did not eschew oaths, they were not strictly a mystery sect, they did not believe, so far as we know, in the regenerative power of baptism, they were far from being pacifists, and so on.[2] There were analogies with the Pharisees, but

[1] To be referred to henceforth by the less equivocal name, Damascus Covenant. The most recent edition is by C. Rabin (2nd ed., Oxford 1957).

[2] Cf. M. Gottstein, *Anti-Essene Traits in the Dead Sea Scrolls* in Vetus Testamentum (=V.T.), iv, (1954) pp. 141–7: also Millar Burrows, pp. 295–293.

The Qumran sect were certainly not the Essenes referred to by Pliny, our only authority for associating the sect with this area: see below, pp. 81–2.

the Qumran *halakha* or code of religious practice was in many respects more severe, comprising moreover significantly different marriage laws and even a different religious calendar.[1] Since then the Qumran sect can have been none of these three, it is not unreasonable to believe (unless there is some valid argument to the contrary) that it was identical with the fourth faction, that of the Zealots. We must therefore re-examine the contemporary sources bearing on the origins and beliefs of this body—once again, to be found primarily in the pages of Josephus—and see whether this assumption is feasible.

What Josephus has to say about the Zealots as a political party is throughout condemnatory: what he has to say about their theoretical basis seems on the surface to be inconsistent. He introduces his famous description of the sects in Judaism (*Wars*, II, viii, 1, §119 ff: cf. also *ibid.*, xvii, 8, §433 and VII, viii, 1, §253) by the statement that the Zealots owed their origin to Judah the Galilaean, who upbraided his countrymen for consenting to pay tribute to the Romans and tolerating mortal masters, after having God for their Lord. The historian goes on to say: 'This man was a sophist who founded a sect of his own, having nothing in common with the others'. (We are justified in deducing from this that the founder of the sect was notorious as a teacher and theoretician.) On the other hand, speaking of this same group elsewhere (*Ant.* XVIII, i, 6 §23) the historian writes that 'while they agree in other respects with the Pharisees, they have an invincible passion for liberty, and take God for their only leader and Lord.' The two statements seem on the surface to be contradictory, and the latter one not wholly self-consistent; for, if the only difference between the Zealots and the Pharisees was political, it hardly seems logical to describe theirs as a 'Fourth Philosophy'.[2] But if

---

[1] The Qumran prohibition of polygamy and of marriage with a niece (recommended as praiseworthy by the Rabbis) makes it certain that there were profound differences between the Sect and the Pharisees, even though their outlook may have approximated in most respects. There is indeed evidence (see elsewhere in this study) that the successive Zealot leaders were remembered sympathetically by the Rabbis of the Talmudic age, and it seems that ultimately the remnant of the Zealots were absorbed by normative Judaism.

[2] The late account of the Zealots in Hippolytus, *Origenis Philosophumena, sive omnium haeresium refutatio*, ix, 26 adds nothing from our point of view. It is perhaps necessary to state that the remarkable article on Zealots in the Jewish Encyclopaedia is largely fanciful and hypothetical. The work by W. R.

we now re-examine Josephus' words, we see that the mis-
understanding is due to a careless reading of what he wrote.
What he states is that on the one hand in their 'philosophy' (i.e.
religious theory) the Zealots were identical with the Pharisees
(that is presumably in their belief in angels, predestination,
the immortality of the soul, bodily resurrection and so on),
except that they refused to admit any human lordship. From
another point of view however the sect could be considered an
independent one, with 'nothing in common with the others'
—i.e. having in certain fundamental respects its own *halakha*,
though to be sure with close Pharisaic analogies.[1] This corresponds faithfully with what we now learn from the literature
found at Qumran, and the difficulty of identifying the Qumran
group with the Zealots disappears.

On this hypothesis, we may now re-examine the entire setting.
It will be seen that no other period, and no other environment, can
reconcile so satisfactorily all the data that we have relating to the
Dead Sea scrolls and the kindred literature, and what was already
known regarding the background of Jewish history at the time of
the Great Revolt, together with the archaeological data and most
of the inferences drawn from them. In other words: we will find
that even without the identification of the Zealot leaders Menahem
or Eleazar with the Teacher of Righteousness, the identification
of their followers at Masadah with the sectaries of the neighbourhood of Qumran gives the only adequate key to the environment
from which this newly-found literature emanated.

The Zealot party was only founded (or became generally

Farmer, *Maccabees, Zealots and Josephus* (Columbia U.P., 1957) approaches the
matter from a different angle, and adds nothing to the subject of our discussion.

Josephus' knowledge of the sect may have been very slight, as indeed his
reticence suggests: we may question whether a person of his character would
have been admitted to their secrets. He states however rather significantly
that they assumed their name—improperly!—not for their political but for
their religious zeal (*Wars*, VII, viii, 1, §270). There are of course similar gaps
in Josephus' accounts of other 'sects': his summary picture of the Pharisees
for example bears little relation to that conveyed in the Rabbinic literature
or even in the New Testament. In fact, what he gives in the *Wars* at least is
not an account of the various Jewish sects, but a slightly elaborated inventory
of them, which serves as foil and pretext for his lengthy and highly idealized
treatise on the Essenes.

[1] C. Rabin, in his new work *Qumran Studies* (Oxford 1957) shows the close
analogies between the doctrines and practises of the Sect and those of Pharisaism, not however so great as to constitute identity.

known), according to Josephus' statement, during the procurator-
ship of Coponius (A.D. 6–9). It is thus obvious that the Zealots
who lived in the Qumran 'monastery' in the last stage of its
occupancy (which ended at the time of the great Revolt against
the Romans) had no immediate connection with the residents
before it was abandoned as a result of the great earthquake in
the spring of 31 B.C. After this, it was left empty for several
years. But here a significant coincidence must be noted. According to the archaeological evidences, the buildings were
reoccupied, again on a semi-monastic basis, in the reign of Herod
Archelaus (4 B.C.–A.D. 6)—precisely that is at the period when
Judah the Galilaean's new party became known in Judaea. We
are driven to the conclusion that the reoccupants in the reign
of Archelaus were Judah the Galilaean and his followers, whose
lives were also organized in a semi-monastic fashion, as we can
see from the Scrolls. The fact that the 'monastery' ruins were
left unoccupied for nearly half a century makes improbable any
direct connection between the later and the earlier denizens,
whose logical course would have been to come back into residence forthwith.[1] No doubt the Zealot sectaries were influenced
by Essene ideas and may even have been joined by some survivors
of the earlier group still living in the neighbourhood. Indeed, it
would be natural to think that to the outside world they appeared
or even posed as Essenes, this providing the cloak for their increasingly subversive activities.[2]

Before the existence of the Zealots as a separate body became
generally known, Judah had been active as an insurgent leader
for some while, following in this the example of his father Hezekiah.[3] In 4 B.C., in the turmoil that succeeded Herod's death,

[1] The reoccupation of abandoned monastic buildings by members of another
'order' was not unknown later: cf. the case of Buckfast Abbey in England.
In Austria, the Benedictine Abbey of Maria Laach stood empty for some years
at the end of the eighteenth and beginning of the nineteenth centuries, then
became a Jesuit convent, and is now Benedictine again.

[2] Some Essenes are said specifically to have identified themselves with the
activist methods of the Zealots (Hippolytus, *Refut. Omn. Haer.* ix, 26, §2).
Cf. also the patriot general John the Essene (*Wars*, II, xx, 4, §567, III, ii,
1, §11 and 2, §19).

[3] There are perhaps vague allusions to Hezekiah, as well as to Menahem his
grandson (see above) in the Talmudic literature, as one not far from their
way of thought. A well-known discussion of the Messianic prophecies (b Sanh.
98b) asserts that they were 'consumed' in the days of Hezekiah (not 'King
Hezekiah') which might conceivably refer to the rebellion of 47 B.C.

he had led one of the revolts in Galilee, where he had occupied Sepphoris and (as his son was to do at Masadah long afterwards) used the armoury in the fortress here to equip his followers, then trying to establish his ascendancy over the other insurgent groups in this region (*Wars*, II, iv, 1, §56). The revolt was soon suppressed by Varus, Legate of Syria, whose friend Gaius captured Sepphoris and reduced the inhabitants to slavery (Ibid., §68). Judah however escaped, as we know, with some of his followers. He now disappears from view for a decade. The documents at our disposal, read in the light of our hypothesis, make it possible to suggest where he spent this period, and what he was doing. It would have been the safest and most natural course for him to take refuge outside the borders of Jewish Palestine, in Syria. Damascus was in fact nearer to Sepphoris than Jerusalem, and the fugitives could very easily have gone underground here for a while, finding help from the teeming and sympathetic Jewish population. To this period may belong the Damascus Covenant, which has so greatly exercised historians.[1] After eight or ten years, the 'Covenanters' returned to Palestine and entered into occupation of the ruined buildings at Qumran.[2] Here (if the suggestion put

---

[1] There is a possible reference to the emigration in the first-century calendar of festive anniversaries, the *Megillat Taanit*, which seems to have a close connection with the milieu of the Qumran community: 'On the seventeenth day of Adar the Gentiles arose up against the remnant of the *saphraya* in the land of Chalcis and Beth Zabdai, but there was deliverance for the House of Israel' [and in consequence it is forbidden to fast on the anniversary]. Chalcis is the area around the sources of the Jordan: Beth Zabdai is N.E. of this, on the road to Damascus. Many years ago Solomon Zeitlin very reasonably conjectured (*Megillat Taanit*, p. 113-4: cf. also L. Ginzberg, *Eine unbekannte jüdische Sekte*, i, 376 f.) that the word ספריא denotes not 'scribes' but 'Sepphorites' or men of Sepphoris. In this case, the reference might well be to the refugees from Sepphoris after its recapture by the Romans and the enslavement of its inhabitants in 4 B.C., when the 'sophist' leader of the revolt, Judah ben Hezekiah, led his followers to Damascus.

[2] The fact that Judah's renewed activity is specifically referred to as taking place 'in Judaea' (not Galilee) might conceivably be an indication that he had by now transferred himself to the south of the country. [I now realise that the logical sequence of events, equally reconcilable with the archaeological and literary evidence, is slightly different from that suggested above. After Judah's abortive rebellion and death in A.D. 6, his followers took up residence for the first time in Qumran, perhaps in the hope of escaping notice in this traditional Essene environment. Judah himself may not therefore have been directly associated with this place.]

With other writers on the subject, I assume the identity of Josephus' sect

forward above is accepted) we have the obvious link between the Covenanters of Damascus and the Qumran sect, which has so earnestly been sought: it is quite unnecessary to suggest that 'Damascus' in these documents has to be interpreted figuratively, or that the name was applied, because of some remote political association, to the area of the Dead Sea also.[1]

Clearly, the Zealots were not to be found only in this region. Indeed, their political programme demanded that they should have adherents as well as propagandists throughout the country. It is to be presumed that Qumran was their 'religious' focus, the centre of their leader's activity and teaching, and the home of those who bound themselves by the strict monastic regime reflected in the Manual of Discipline. Possibly, there may have been some other Zealot establishments of the same type in the neighbourhood. But throughout the country there would naturally have been large numbers of sympathizers, some more and some less closely identified with the Qumran outlook and way of life. These would inevitably have become increasingly prominent on the outbreak of the revolt against the Romans in A.D. 66. Even now, however, there were obvious differences between the strict 'monastic' Zealots under Eleazar ben Jair in the Dead Sea region and their sympathisers elsewhere in the country, some (or most) of them collaborating unreservedly with the mass of the patriot forces.

Judah did not long survive the return to Palestine. 'In the days of the taxing' (Acts v, 37) under Quirinius he 'induced

---

of the 'Fourth Philosophy' with the Zealots, as seems inevitable. A slight change of vocabulary only is necessary if this obvious deduction is not admitted: it is a distinction without a difference.

[1] The assumption that the Damascus Covenant was not drawn up in Damascus (cf. R. North, *The Damascus of Qumran Geography* in Palestine Exploration Quarterly (=P.E.Q.), 1955, pp. 34–38: I. Rabinowitz, *A Reconsideration of 'Damascus' and '390 Years' in the 'Damascus' ('Zadokite') Fragment* in J.B.L. xxiii, 11–35), is a typical instance of the modern tendency to assume that ancient texts mean anything but what they appear to say. The text of the documents is perfectly clear: they speak in plain terms (vi, 5) of 'the Repentant of Israel who went forth from the land of Judah and dwelled in the land of Damascus' (not therefore in some area of Judaea which by an exercise of ingenuity might be assumed to be in the Damascus orbit) but apparently were no longer there. The sequel is indicated in *The War of the Sons of Light and Sons of Darkness* (i. 3), where we are told how the former came from the Wilderness of the Gentiles to dwell in the Wilderness of Jerusalem.

multitudes of Jews to refuse to register' (*Wars*, VII, viii, 1, §253) on the ground that thereby they would recognize Roman suzerainty. Apparently he perished in the subsequent disorders.[1] The next we hear of the party is the crucifixion of his two sons, Simon and Jacob, in A.D. 46–8, as already noticed. The surviving brother, Menahem, now emerges as the head of the party. We are not informed of his activity in the period that immediately followed. It is reasonable to assume that he lived obscurely, in some remote and sparsely-inhabited part of the country, perhaps further elaborating his teachings to his followers. The Desert of Judah was obviously suited for the purpose. This confirms the possibility that, after its reoccupation in the reign of Herod Archelaus, Qumran may have been the Zealot centre, where their teacher developed his doctrines and his disciples perhaps copied his writings. It was here presumably that Menahem now organized the Sicarii, whom he sent out to perform their deeds of daring (*Wars*, II, xiii, 3, §§254–7: VII, viii, 1, §§254–5); the situation is not unlike that of the Assassins in their Syrian fastnesses in the twelfth and thirteenth centuries. The fact that Menahem and his followers were able to seize Masadah in A.D. 66 suggests that they had their centre of operations in that neighbourhood; in Galilee, there would have been other equally important objectives nearer to hand.

On the basis of archaeological evidence it has been suggested that the second occupation of the monastery at Qumran, begun under Herod Archelaus, ended in A.D. 68, when presumably it was captured .by Vespasian in the course of the expedition to the Dead Sea, during which he carried out the barbarous experiment described by Josephus. The evidence for this is that the coin-sequence ends with five coins of the third year of the First Revolt (A.D. 68–9). This however is only approximately conclusive. As with the Roman advance conditions in the south of the country became more difficult, so communications with the outside world were more restricted, and newly-minted coins need

---

[1] A possible mention of Judah the Galilaean in a very favourable light may also occur in the Talmudic literature (Midrash Ecclesiastes Rabba, I, 30) where the name of 'Judah ben Hezekiah' is mentioned as that of a neglected scholar, whom God would one day bring out of his obscurity. Ginzberg (*Commentary on Palestinian Talmud*, I, 340) reads Judah *and* Hezekiah, referring the passage to the two sons of R. Hiyya. Yet even if the correction is justified, the form in which the tradition was preserved may be the result of retentive folk-memory.

not necessarily have been brought to the monastery, and still less lost there. Hence Qumran may not have fallen during Vespasian's expedition in A.D. 68, but perhaps during that led by Flavius Silva in A.D. 73, when Masadah was captured. The matter is of no great importance, except that it makes possible to extend the period when the cult of Menahem's memory was cherished by his disciples at Qumran for as many as seven or eight years, from A.D. 66 to A.D. 73. If for example it is true that the reference in the Commentary on Habakkuk to the enemy practice of sacrificing to their standards refers specifically to the action of the Roman legionaries after the capture of Jerusalem,[1] it would be an additional argument for the slightly later dating of the fall of this spiritual stronghold.[2] It is surely significant in this connection that the buildings at Qumran are said to partake of the nature of a fortress as well as of a monastery. The basic literature of the Zealot party could thus be the product of a period of some three-quarters of a century, from the time when the 'sophist' Judah first organized it as a separate body in the first decade of the Christian era, down to the period of the Jewish revolt, and even as late as A.D. 73.

The picture that our hypothesis suggests is fantastic in modern terms, to be sure: a 'sect' predominantly male, most of them hardened soldiers and far from averse to the shedding of blood, though at the same time professing advanced ideals of social justice; holding bizarre religious doctrines which they were prepared to defend to their last breath; fighting simultaneously against the foreign enemy without and no less bitterly against religious adversaries within (to the outside observer, only a whit less extreme and bizarre than they were themselves); daily anticipating the Divine intervention to save their people, once it

[1] The discussions are summarized by Rowley, *The Zadokite Fragments and the Dead Sea Scrolls*, pp. 72-5, and in P.E.Q., 1956, pp. 97-105. The evidence that the events of 70 are specifically referred to is emphatically maintained by Prof. Driver. There is clearly no compelling argument against this, and in the light of the material assembled above it seems certain. Moreover, even though vague parallels can be assembled from other times and areas, it may be assumed that the writer of the Commentary was not particularly interested with what went on in Syria or Rome, whereas he was vitally concerned with what had happened in Jerusalem. For further apparent references to the period A.D. 68-70 in the Qumran literature see below p. 35 ff.

[2] It is not suggested that Qumran was a military stronghold, which Josephus need have mentioned in *Wars*, IV, ix, 9, §555, among those which held out after the rest of Judaea was overrun.

returned to God wholeheartedly (that is, in accordance with their own views), when they would issue triumphantly to overwhelm their enemies in the field; and meanwhile practising military exercises, composing religious manifestos, drawing up Utopian constitutions, recording personal grudges against half-hearted supporters and writing part-mystical and part-practical tactical handbooks, in which the pious inscriptions to be embroidered on the banners of the various detachments were described with the same enthusiasm as the weapons which they were to bear in combat. Preposterous as this might seem to the modern mind, one can imagine it very well in (for example) the England of the seventeenth century, when the Fifth Monarchy Men under Thomas Venner were composed of enthusiasts who had acquitted themselves splendidly in the field under Cromwell in the New Model armies, but subsequently withdrew themselves into belligerent aloofness, published a series of fantastic military pamphlets and plotted a military coup d'état which would establish the Rule of Christ on earth.[1]

Even so, is it plausible that during the tragic period of the siege of Jerusalem and after the fall of the Holy City the Zealot extremists can have remained calmly at Qumran, peacefully studying their doctrines and still copying or even composing their literature? The answer is emphatically 'Yes'. For if those in authority in Jerusalem represented the powers of darkness among the Jewish people, the nearer they approached to disaster the more imminent the great Divine deliverance obviously was. Hence the fall of Jerusalem, instead of dashing the hopes of the sectaries, necessarily raised them to a fever-pitch: one can well imagine that from time to time the excited sectarian leader demonstrated to his followers (some of whom in turn may have set down his assertions in writing) how all that was happening conformed to

[1] The Zealot outlook is exactly reflected in a passage of the Day of Atonement (and New Year) liturgy: 'Give then glory, O Lord, to Thy people . . . confidence to them that wait for Thee . . . speedily in our days. Then shall the righteous see and be glad, and the upright shall exult, and the pious triumph in jubilation . . . when Thou shalt wipe the Wicked Empire from the Land, and Thou shalt reign alone . . . on Mount Zion . . . and in Jerusalem Thy holy city'. (The phrase 'The Wicked Empire' is currently interpreted as 'The Dominion of Arrogance', and in many rites modified in that sense.) It is not suggested that this passage is of Zealot authorship, but they would hardly have expressed differently their creed, of the imminent triumph of the monotheistic ideal coupled with political deliverance.

Prophecy, and hence made Redemption nearer and even more certain. Disillusionment came only with the siege and capture of Masadah in A.D. 73, so graphically described by Josephus, when Eleazar ben Jair at last faced reality and died by his own hand, together with his devoted followers.[1]

A great deal of the literature from Qumran revolves about the conception of the 'End of Days'. If as formerly proposed these documents date back to the second century B.C., they would presumably refer to a remote future, being in the accepted sense 'eschatological'. But more careful reading, in the light of what has been said above, shows clearly that this is not the case. The 'End of Days' as envisaged in these documents was something certain, practical, and above all, at that time, imminent. We are at the period of the great Revolt against Rome and the Siege of Jerusalem, when the Holy Land was being overrun by the hosts of the idol-worshippers, as the inspired heathen prophet Balaam had foretold would happen at the End of Days (Numbers xxv, 14 ff.), and the backsliders of Israel were being annihilated. The small, chosen band of those who served God aright were in daily expectation of His intervention to save them, overwhelming the rule of iniquity and establishing His sovereignty on earth. The 'End of Days' when the Teacher of Righteousness had already made his appearance was now, and the Qumran literature breathes the feverish confidence of this expectant period.[2]

We can go further. This being the End of Days, it was the period to which Bible prophecy looked and on which Bible prophecy centred, if it could be rightly interpreted. It was apparently therefore a cardinal principle of the Sect that *all* or most of the Old Testament prophecies—or at least those not specifically referring to some event of ancient history—must therefore refer to the now-unfolding End of Days—that is, to the events, circumstances and immediate prospects of the second

---

[1] The pathetic persistence of the Sect in the face of what would appear to others the most utter disillusionment has sufficient parallel in history at other times. For example: although Joanna Southcott died in hypothetical Messianic pregnancy in 1814, her adherents are still producing a constant stream of enthusiastic literature in 1958.

[2] For this reason, the phrase עד עמוד מורה צדק באחרית הימים (Damascus Covenant VI, 11) certainly does not imply the Resurrection of the Teacher of Righteousness at the end of time (as it has been made to do, with the most sensational implications), but simply: 'until the rise of the Teacher, in the (present) apocalyptic days'.

half of the first century of the Christian era. Moreover, the head of the Sect had been inspired by God with the power of under-standing and interpreting these allusions, as is clearly stated in the Habakkuk commentary, ii, 8–9: 'The Priest in whose heart God has given wisdom to explain (לפשור) all the words of His servants the prophets, through whose hand God has recounted all that is coming on His people and His land'. Whether here the term Priest indicated the Teacher of Righteousness Menahem, or his successor in the leadership of the sect Eleazar, who set down and developed his conceptions, is not quite certain. Which-ever the case, it was this that gave the leader of the sect his unique quality, putting him too on a level with the Prophets —and at the same time ingeniously making possible a continuation of the prophetic spirit without adding to the accepted canon of the Scriptural prophetic writings.[1] This literary work was obviously a main preoccupation and occupation at Qumran in our period, constantly perhaps being revised and supplemented as fresh events suggested new parallels. Of this literature, we have one specimen in tolerably complete state on the Book of Habakkuk, fragments of others on Hosea, Isaiah, Nahum, Micah, Zephaniah and (selected?) Psalms.[2] To apply the term 'Commentary' to these compositions is not quite correct (though

[1] It is noteworthy how in similar circumstances the religious mind may react in an identical manner even after two thousand years. The Zealots in the first century thought in the same fashion as some of the disciples of Joanna South-cott in the nineteenth, of whom we read in a recent work (G. R. Balleine, *Past Finding Out* (1957, p. 95) that they held that: 'The Scriptures are not History, but figures of what is to come. All that is said of Isaac and Jacob etc. are prophecies in parabolic form to foretell future events. . . . Though the writers seem to speak of transactions past, they are foretelling future events. . . . Since all events described in the Bible were to happen in the Last Days, and since every [adherent] believed that the Last Days had begun, it followed that the whole Bible drama would take place in his own lifetime'. Much of this could be applied in identical terms to the period and persons now under consideration.

[2] For details of publication see below, p.38 note. That these expositions originally covered the entirety of the Biblical books here in question, as is generally assumed, is problematical. It is not unlikely that the Teacher com-posed and transmitted such glosses only when he discerned in the text some allusion to the 'End of Days' which was unfolding itself before his eyes. The protracted *pešer* on Habakkuk would thus be an exception: the glosses to the other books may have been isolated jottings, or may have constituted portions of a florilegium, such as has in fact been found. In this case, the Qumran literature was a good deal less extensive than is generally believed.

to be sure there is little alternative) nor are they in the category of 'midrash' (Professor Solomon Zeitlin has emphasised not without reason that both of these conceptions are anachronistic for the period). The *pešer* is neither the one nor the other, but the inspired application of the terms of the Biblical prophecies to the 'End of Days' which had already begun. It follows (what was already indeed becoming sufficiently obvious) that most of the events referred to in these glosses must necessarily belong to this period, reflecting the outlook, the personalities, the events and the background of the great Revolt against Roman rule.

Our central hypothesis makes it easy to understand, moreover, what has hitherto remained a matter of perplexity, why the Scrolls were hidden. If Qumran was the original centre, and remained the scriptorium and propaganda-centre of the Zealot brotherhood, a great number of manuscript works were no doubt in existence there or were still being copied or compiled—apart from ancient texts, some perhaps taken over from the earlier inmates or brought into the monastery when the surrounding area was overrun by the Romans. (The suggestion has been made[1] that some of the Biblical manuscripts may have been brought thither from the Temple in Jerusalem.) When the menace to Qumran itself became imminent, perhaps as late as the winter of A.D. 72–3, the entire 'library'—including perhaps some unfinished works—was put by the inhabitants into hiding-places among the caves which honeycombed the surrounding cliffs, before their withdrawal to Masadah or elsewhere. For they were perfectly assured that this was the 'End of Days', that God was about to manifest himself in all His glory to vouchsafe victory to the remnant of His people, and that glorious triumph would not long be delayed. They placed the manuscripts into concealment calmly and systematically, confident that before long they would be able to return and retrieve them. One unfinished work might well have been the Commentary on Habakkuk, which as we have seen contains allusions to events as recent as A.D. 66, or even A.D. 70, and which covers only two out of the three chapters of the Biblical book: the manuscript ends indeed somewhat abruptly. Conceivably the writer of the work did not have the conclusion in the text before him, but that he could not see apocalyptic and messianic allusions in the third chapter is out of the question—the writers of the mediaeval liturgical Targumim

[1] Cf. Rengstorf in *Allgem. jüd. Zeitschr.* for 15th March 1957, p. 21.

revelled in it. That he left the work unfinished, when Qumran was abandoned, seems at least an equally plausible explanation.[1]

One further point that emerges must be emphasised. Obviously, the Qumran literature illustrates the religious atmosphere of Judaea in the first century of the Christian era, out of which Christianity emerged. But there is not an iota of reasonable evidence in support of the theory on which so much ink has been spilled and· to which so much argumentation has been devoted— that we have here the case, a century or two centuries before the time of Jesus, of a religious teacher who was martyred—even crucified—and then rose again. The episode of the Teacher of Righteousness belongs to the generation after, not before, the Crucifixion of Jesus. It is hard to read any idea of resurrection into the sources, the 'End of Days' when the Teacher 'rose' (not 'rose again') being the present apocalyptic times. If there is any reciprocal influence, it is obviously in the reverse direction —for the emphasis placed on the story of the epiphany of the Teacher in the Temple immediately before his violent death may improbably though conceivably be influenced by the Christian reports of the solemn appearance of Jesus in the Temple before his Passion. This similarity is indeed so slight as to be negligible. That the story anticipated, or influenced, the birth of Christianity simply does not come into question.

It must be emphasised that our identification of the central character in the Dead Sea Scrolls, upon which this wider argumentation is based, does not turn merely on the report of the judicial assassination or persecution of a prominent person in Judaea in the relevant period. The episode concerned a σοφιστής —i.e. Teacher—who suffered at the hands of one whose essential quality was that of being a *priest*, and whose sect continued to exist afterwards *near the Dead Sea*; further, the two episodes took place at the same time of the Jewish religious year, and both

[1] Our hypothesis may moreover explain one curious feature regarding the Biblical texts found at Qumran. It is stated that portions of all the books of the Hebrew Old Testament have been found in the Caves, with the solitary exception of the Book of Esther. Since the recital of this book, from a written scroll (like the Pentateuch) was obligatory in Tannaitic times, this absence is puzzling. But the Book of Esther is the only book of the Old Testament in which alien rule and the supreme authority of a pagan King are specifically, emphatically, and even adulatorily admitted. It would not therefore be remarkable were the Book not accepted by a sect which recognized God alone as King.

the one and the other victim formerly had a follower of the same name. These are the details that raise this identification beyond conjecture. As a logical consequence of this, it is possible to make in this paper a number of other suggestions towards the reconstruction of Jewish history in the first century. But even if these should not be accepted, the validity of the main thesis would be unaffected.

As far as the palaeographical problem is concerned, the present arguments provide, in the case of the majority of the documents, only a *terminus ad quem* for their chronology. The exact dating of the Habakkuk Commentary has no necessary bearing for example on the Biblical codices, and there is no reason whatsoever why some of these should not be two or even four centuries earlier. As for the original literature, there is nothing to show that, in some cases it may not be of similar antiquity, and it could well contain historical allusions which may range back throughout history. Hence even the most unmistakable reference to circumstances of (say) the early Maccabaean period in no way invalidates the ascription of the Habakkuk *pešer* and the related works to the first century A.D.[1]

VI

In view of the identification of persons, period and circumstances put forward here, much of the literature of the Qumran sect begins to appear in a clearer light, and many references hitherto obscure become plain. Some preliminary suggestions only will be made at this point.

The so-called 'War of the Sons of Light and Sons of Dark-

---

[1] This has become certain with the recently-announced discovery of fresh fragments bearing names which have been read as Hyrcan ... (i.e. Hyrcanus II, 63–40 B.C.?), Aemilius (i.e. Pompey's lieutenant in Syria, Paulus Aemilius?) and as it seems also Shelom-Zion the Queen (i.e. Salome Alexandra, 76–67 B.C.). If these readings are correct, we have now in the Dead Sea fragments a series of names which (including those of Demetrius and Antiochus mentioned below, pp. 41–2) cover a period of approximately a century and a half. Obviously, this cannot assist in pin-pointing the period of the episode of the Teacher of Righteousness! All that can be deduced from these fragments (which no doubt will be supplemented from time to time) is that the Qumran literature belongs to a period later than Pompey's invasion, when the memory of the Hasmonaean monarchy was not dead.

ness'[1] speaks for example almost at the outset (i, 2) of the 'Kittim' of Asshur (=Syria) and, immediately after (i, 4) of the 'Kittim' of Egypt, whose armies also were to be defeated by the Sons of Light. This politico-geographical duplication could not very well apply to any Near Eastern power before the Romans, and even in the Roman period, when Judaea was generally subordinated to the province of Syria, it would not normally have been natural. But in preparing for his Palestinian campaign, Vespasian first concentrated his forces in Syria, marching on Palestine from the north: meanwhile he sent his son Titus to Egypt to bring up the fifteenth legion from the South (*Wars*, III, i, 3, §§6–8). Here we have, it seems, the Kittim of Asshur and the Kittim of Egypt.[2] The two forces converged at Ptolemais, which was to be the base for the campaign, and whence the legions marched inland (*ibid*. ii, 4, §29; iv, 2, §§64–9). A fragmentary *pešer* on Isaiah x, 28 ff. describing the War of the Kittim, speaks of the End of Days when he (the identity of the subject of the verb is obscure) 'goeth up from the Plain of Acco to fight . . .'[3] The editor explains this as being the route of the Messiah, but the lemma, which deals with the advance of the impious Assyrians on the Holy City, shows that this cannot be the case. An alternative suggestion has been made, that the reference is to the War of Gog and Magog,[4] though to provide a precise way-bill for Messianic days is somewhat ludicrous. In the light of what has been said above, the obvious interpretation is that this passage refers to the concentration of the invading Roman forces in the Plain of Acco (=Ptolemais) just described. This is so obvious as almost to suggest without corroboratory evidence the approximate dating of some at least of this literature at the time of the Revolt.

The Habakkuk commentary (iv, 10 ff.) speaks of the rapid sequence of the rulers of the Kittim, who 'by the counsel of a guilty house pass, the one before the other, and come one after the other to destroy the [land].' This would appear to be a transparent reference to the sequence of Roman Emperors

---

[1] Latest edition, very amply annotated, by Y. Yadin (revised impression Jerusalem 1957).

[2] See G. R. Driver in Journal of Theological Studies (=J.T.S.) n.s. vii, 262–3: there is no need here to elaborate this point further.

[3] Published by J. Allegro in J.B.L., lxxv, 178.

[4] Millar Burrows in V.T., vii, 35–61.

after the violent death of Nero in A.D. 68, 'The Year of Five Emperors', when Galba, Vitellius, Otto and Vespasian were all raised to the purple in rapid succession.[1] A fragment of a *florilegium* found in the fourth cave quotes Joshua's curse on the man who should rebuild Jericho (Josh. vi, 26), adding the gloss: 'And behold a man accursed, a man of Belial, shall arise to be a snare to his people and destruction to all his neighbours, and he shall arise . . . that the two of them may be instruments of violence. And they shall return and build the . . . (and will) establish for it walls and towers, to provide a refuge of wickedness . . . in Israel and a horrible thing in Ephraim and in Judah. (And they) shall cause pollution in the land, and great contempt among the sons of. . . . Blood like water on the rampart of the daughter of Zion and in the boundary of Jerusalem'.[2] This could well be a reference to Vespasian's capture of Jericho in 68, though there is no need to insist on this point.

Meanwhile the Zealot communities at Qumran and Masadah managed to maintain themselves in spite of increasing difficulties. The fragmentary *pešer* on Psalm xxxvii speaks of the Repentant in the wilderness whom God sustained in time of famine, whereas those who failed to follow them suffered (as was indeed the case with the beleaguered inhabitants of Jerusalem) from hunger and sickness. In the fourth cave, according to the summary reports[3] there has been found a fragmentary scroll giving 'some liturgical lamentations over Jerusalem, which owe much to the biblical but are not identical'. To amplify the Lamentations of Jeremiah while the Temple was still standing was unnecessary. Hence, unless this document belongs to the period 168–5 B.C. precisely, it is natural to ascribe it to a period immediately after the summer of A.D. 70.[4] Mention has already been made of the

[1] The point is elaborated by Prof. Driver, *ut supra*.

[2] J.B.L. lxxv, 185–6. The execrated Builder of Jericho might be Herod, who erected there a palace and public buildings, including an amphitheatre —perhaps the 'refuge of wickedness' of the gloss.

[3] R.B. lxiii, 49–67; Biblical Archaeologist, xix, 75–96.

[4] The Roman triumph is apparently referred to also in the fragment of the florilegium published by Allegro (J.B.L., lxxv, pp. 179–80) in which Isaiah x, 34 ('And he shall cut down the thickets of the forest with iron, and Lebanon shall fall by a mighty one') is interpreted as a reference to the warriors of the Kittim, which is followed by an allusion to flight from Jerusalem. It is noteworthy that according to the Talmudic legend this verse was quoted by R. Johanan ben Zakkai when he was brought before Vespasian(!) after his escape from the beleaguered city (b Gittin 56 a–b). Conceivably this is an

apparent, much-discussed reference in the commentary on Habakkuk to the sacrifices offered by the legionaries to their standards in the precincts of the Temple after the fall of Jerusalem.[1]

Our documents allude more than once to the Last Priest, or Priests. He, and they are spoken of coolly, but without rancour, and it seems impossible therefore to identify this Last Priest with the Wicked Priest. An isolated gloss on Hosea for example refers to 'the Last Priest who stretched forth his hand to smite Ephraim.'[2] This in itself is unintelligible, but it is clearly to be brought into relation with a statement in the *pešer* on Psalm xxxvii, 14–5: 'Its interpretation concerns the Wicked Ones of Ephraim and Manasseh who will seek to stretch forth their hand against the Priest and the men of his Council in the time of testing that is coming upon them. And God will redeem them from their hand, and afterwards they shall be given into the hand of the Terrible Ones of the Gentiles for judgement.' Far from being eschatological, this passage seems to convey an almost explicit reference to well-established contemporary events. The only time in the entire period of the Second Temple (not merely in that under present consideration) when persons who can rationally be identified with the inhabitants of Ephraim and Manasseh may be said to have played a role in the affairs of the nation as a whole was after the capitulation of Jotapata and Vespasian's conquest of Galilee in A.D. 68.[3]

---

echo of Qumran Zealot exegesis. Similarly, the picture of the Messianic banquet in which grace is recited first by the Priest, then by the Messiah, then by the rest of the congregation (*Discoveries in the Judaean Desert*, i, 108 ff.) is parallelled in the Talmudic passage (b Pes. 119b) in which we are informed that Abraham passes the cup of Benediction to Isaac and Isaac to David; and in Midrash Rabba, Exodus xxv, where it is passed in turn from God to the archangel Michael, then to Gabriel, then to the patriarchs, then to Moses. It is obvious that this was a popular imagery.

[1] See above p. 29.

[2] The fragmentary 'commentaries' to be referred to here and in the following pages have been published as follows: on Nahum, by Allegro in J.B.L. lxxv, 90–93 (with a tiny fragment on Hosea, p. 93): on Psalm xxxvii by the same scholar, *ibid.*, pp. 94–5, and in P.E.Q., lxxxvi. 69–75; on Micah, Zephaniah, and Psalms lvii, lxviii by Milik in *Discoveries in the Judaean Desert*, i, 77–82 (the first originally in *Revue Biblique* (=R.B.), lix, 412–8). It will be unnecessary to repeat these references.

[3] Clearly, this passage cannot refer to any period before the Judaisation of Galilee under John Hyrcanus (135–104), or even some while afterwards, as time was needed before the process became effective. Nor can the reference be to the Samaritans, whose Israelite stock was strenuously denied by the Jews

The intransigent refugees from the north of the country ('Ephraim and Manasseh') now streamed south under John of Gischala (Josephus' former opponent) and began to assume a preponderant role in Jerusalem, dominating its political life and suppressing any possibility of compromise with the enemy. Among their rivals in the leadership of the war-party was the Zealot chieftain, Eleazar ben Simon, who had entrenched himself in the Temple, and was able to control the ceremonies there. The High Priest at the time was Phineas (Phanni) ben Samuel, a country stone-mason who had recently been chosen by lot for his high office, to the horror of the aristocratic and traditional faction (*Wars*, IV, iii, 8, §§155–7). Appointment to all office by lot, an egalitarian and 'democratic' policy throughout the ancient world, was specifically stipulated by the Qumran zealot code (Discipline Manual, iv, 26, v, 3, cf. vi, 16–21, ix, 7–8). Phineas was there-fore the Zealot nominee and (since he officiated in the Temple) closely associated with Eleazar ben Simon the Zealot leader, who was in control there. Between their followers and those of John of Gischala a constant guerilla warfare now raged. Here then we surely have the 'Last Priest' (he was, in fact, the last High Priest) who was at war with the 'Wicked of Ephraim and Manasseh'.[1] The identification seems to be made the more prob-able by the reference in the Commentary on Habakkuk (ix, 4–7) to 'the last Priests of Jerusalem, who gather wealth and booty from the spoil of the gentiles. But in the End of Days their wealth with their spoil will be given into the hands of the hosts of the Kittim': Josephus (*Wars*, II, xx, 3, §564) specifically informs us that Eleazar ben Simon owed his power to the fact that he had in his hands the Roman spoils, the money taken from Cestius, and a great part of the public treasure—all destined presumably to be recaptured in due course, when Jerusalem fell.[2] In the end, Eleazar's party and their High Priestly nominee were defeated

---

at this time. The title 'Ephraim and Manasseh' would naturally be applied to the inhabitants of the former northern monarchy, without reference to tribal boundaries.

[1] For John of Gischala's 'wicked' deeds, see below. But it would be cha-racteristic of the Qumran literature to refer to ritual transgressions, and it is interesting to note how Josephus (*Wars*, V, xiii, 6, §§564–5; VII, viii, 1, §§263–4) emphasizes the fact that his enemy was careless about religious observances.

[2] It is worth while to emphasize the precision of the language of the Qumran writer. The Wicked Priest enriched himself both from spoil and *from the property of the cities of Judah* (Habakkuk Commentary xi, 8–10; xii, 9–10),

but not overwhelmed by John of Gischala's followers (once again, on a holyday, when some calendarical disparity may have been involved, facilitating the victory: *Wars*, V, iii, 1, §98 ff). But, on this occasion, unusual moderation was to be shown. The defeated faction now joined the ranks of their former opponents (*ibid.*, vi, 1, §250) their lives being spared: they were thus 're-deemed by God' as stated in the gloss on Psalm xxxvii quoted above. On the other hand, the victors were in due course to be 'delivered over into the hands of the Terrible Ones of the Gentiles for judgement', the redoubtable John of Gischala being sentenced to perpetual imprisonment by the Romans after their triumph (*Ibid.*, VI, ix, 4, §§433–4; VII, v, 3, §118).

The gloss on Hosea v. 15 cited above contrasts, perhaps punningly, the Last Priest (כוהן האחרון) and the Lion of Wrath (כפיר החרון), who may thus be this Priest's principal opponent, John of Gischala. Indeed, it is a graphic and fitting description of that fiery, uncompromising, merciless fighter for Jewish independence.

This character, however, figures most significantly in the fragmentary *pešer*, on Nahum ii, 13: '*The Lion tears sufficient for his whelps, and strangles for his lionesses prey*: Its interpretation concerns the Lion of Wrath, who smote with his mighty and the men of his counsel. '*And he filled [his caves with prey] and his den with ravine*: Its interpretation concerns the Lion of Wrath . . . death on the Interpreters of Smooth Things, who hangs men up alive [which was never done?] in Israel before.' The gloss goes on to interpret the prey of the Lion of Wrath as the 'wealth which the priests of Jerusalem gathered together'.[1] 'To hang men up alive' has been interpreted as 'to crucify',[2] and the passage has been associated with the crucifixion of his opponents by Alexander Jannaeus. But the reference to Jannaeus is hypothetical, while as we have seen there is solid ground for identifying the Lion of Wrath with John of Gischala. Moreover, to 'hang men up alive' may but does not necessarily refer to crucifixion. On the

---

whereas the Last Priest specifically gathered *the wealth of the Gentiles* (ix, 4–5). From *Wars*, IV, iv, 1, §225, it appears that Eleazar ben Simon was himself a Priest. The Tosephta too states that Phineas was elected by lot.

[1] Unfortunately the fragment is so defective that it is impossible to reconstruct the text satisfactorily, almost one half of every line being absent.

[2] Allegro's interpretation is accepted by Wieder, Journal of Jewish Studies (=J.J.S.), vii, 71–2.

other hand, Josephus informs us in horrified terms of the executions carried out under John of Gischala's orders during the
siege of Jerusalem (*Wars*, V, x, 4, §§439–41; VII, viii, 1, §263):
'The men of rank and wealth on the other hand were brought
up to the tyrants. Of them some were falsely accused of conspiracy
and executed, as were others on the charge of betraying the city
to the Romans. . . . They pledged each other in turn in the citizens'
blood, and shared the carcasses of their unfortunate victims.' (That
crucifixion was included among the penalties is not excluded:
in fact since the Romans crucified fugitives from the city, the
desperate patriot commander may well have inflicted the same
penalty by way of deterrent on the deserters whom he punished
so relentlessly: *Wars*, V, x, 4, §§439–40; xi, 1, §§449–51).[1] There
is good reason to believe that among those against whom action
was now taken, on the grounds that they favoured capitulation,
were the Pharisaic leaders. It will be recalled that at this stage
R. Johanan ben Zakkai had himself smuggled out of the city on
a bier, later making his way to the enemy camp; the Pharisaic
leader Simon ben Gamaliel, who had played a prominent part
at the outset of the Revolution, now disappears from view, and
is conjectured to have suffered death: while the Secretary of
the *Boule* (*i.e.* Sanhedrin) is known to have been executed
(*Wars* V, xiii, 1, §532). In the cryptic language of the literature
from Qumran, the Pharisees seem to be designated as דורשי
חלקות (i.e. 'Makers of Smooth [or Easy] Interpretations' rather
than 'Seekers after Smooth Things') and the passage of the commentary just quoted may refer to the attacks now made on them:
the writer half-approved of the executions, but not of their manner.
For the Pharisees had a tradition of political compromise almost
from the beginning of the Maccabaean period, which is referred
to in the previous passage ('*Whither the lion went, to bring there
a young lion*'. . . . Its interpretation concerns (Demet)rius king of
Greece, who desired to enter Jerusalem through the plot of the
Makers of Smooth Interpretations'). This event apparently took
place well before the appearance of the Kings of the Kittim,
and has been associated with the invitation extended by the

---

[1] Even assuming that the Editor's reconstruction of the text is justified,
the fact that Alexander Jannaeus perpetrated the same cruelty more than a
century before has no bearing whatsoever on the matter. Even today pam-
phleteers do not hesitate to qualify as 'unprecedented' unpopular practices
which are within recent memory.

Pharisees to Demetrius III[1] of Syria in the reign of Alexander Jannaeus.[2]

We are left with another principal character of the documents from Qumran as yet unidentified. It is pointless and in some ways ludicrous to attempt to determine all allusions and personalities in such literature. Our historical records are limited: and persons who may have loomed very prominently in the eyes of the groups on the shores of the Dead Sea may have made no impact whatsoever outside, and still less be mentioned in the writings of the historian on whom we have to rely for nearly all of our information. Nevertheless, it is worth while to see whether there is in our sources any person who fulfils the conditions. We read in the commentary on Habakkuk of the Man of Lies (איש הכזב) who (II, 1–2) did not fully believe in the words of the Teacher of Righteousness which came from God; and (V, 11–14) rejected the Law, and quarrelled with the Teacher of Righteousness on the occasion when the latter did not receive proper help from the House of Absalom. In the Damascus Covenant (xx, 15) we are told that about forty years would elapse between the time of

---

[1] It is not germane to the purpose of the present paper to dispute this identification, but one may observe that Demetrius III did not in fact play a role of very great significance in Jewish history. It is therefore more logical to identify the ruler in question (cf. Rowley, *Jewish Apocalyptic and the Dead Sea Scrolls*, 1957, p. 26) with Demetrius I, who in 162 B.C. seized the Syrian throne from the infant son of Antiochus Epiphanes and embarked on a vigorous but conciliatory policy in Judaea. His general Bacchides persuaded the Pietists in Jerusalem to accept Alcimus as High Priest: later, Demetrius came to an agreement with the Hasmonaeans, who recognized his suzerainty while receiving a guarantee of religious freedom. Obviously, this recognition of foreign rule was in opposition to the cardinal Zealot creed, and may in their eyes have been the beginning of the débâcle from which the Jewish people was to be saved by the 'End of Days'.

If either Demetrius is called King of Greece (the name is anyhow incomplete in the fragment, and the reconstruction problematical), the term Kittim cannot possibly denote the Greek rulers, as some scholars still assert. Attention may perhaps be called to the appearance in Vespasian's armies beneath the walls of Jerusalem of another Antiochus Epiphanes, son of King Antiochus IV of Commagene (*Wars*, V, xi, 3, §§460–1 etc.).

[2] This passage is complicated and difficult to explain. As Rabin says (J.J.S., vii, 11) the fact that Demetrius' name is mentioned suggests that Jannaeus' reign was not the time of the appearance of the Teacher of Righteousness. My impression is that the writer may have been engaged in building up an indictment against the Pharisees back to their first emergence as a separate sect. But no definite conclusion can be based on an isolated and mutilated fragment.

the death of the Teacher of the sect (the title 'Teacher of Righteousness' is not used on this occasion) and the passing of all the
men of war who went with 'the Man of Lies'.

There is a known historical personality who seems to fulfil
the requirements. Simon bar Giora first emerges at the outset
of the revolt against the Romans in 66, when in a brilliant action
he cut off Cestius' baggage train at Beth Horon and brought it
back to Jerusalem. Clearly, there was adequate opportunity for
him to have been in contact at this time with Menahem, the
Zealot military leader. Ardently patriotic; belonging it seems
to the 'depressed elements' (for Bar Giora means 'the Son of the
Proselyte'); and with an advanced social programme (later he
was to plunder the wealthy and release the slaves); he clearly
shared many views with Menahem's followers, but he was not
won over. Simon's egalitarian activities subsequently became so
pronounced that the central administration in Jerusalem sent
an army against him, and he took refuge with his followers in
Masadah. The two bodies however did not merge, which suggests
that there must have been some friction. (The fact that his following included women (*Wars*, IV, ix, 3, §505) may have offended
the ascetic discipline of his hosts.)[1] In due course Bar Giora led
his forces (as mentioned above) to Jerusalem, where he took a
heroic part in the defence of the city in its last days. He and his
followers could presumably have coalesced fully with the Qumran
sectaries only if they had completely accepted the latter's programme and ideas, which they refused to do ('They did not
believe in the words of the Teacher of Righteousness which came
from God'). In fact, Bar Giora obviously had his own social
and perhaps religious programme, this justifying in the eyes of
the Sect his qualification as 'the Man of Lies';[2] and this is the

---

[1] Yadin (*War of the Sons of Light &c.*, pp. 62–7, 227) calls attention to the
fact that the Qumran sect, while not celibate, objected to the presence of
women in the camp during a campaign.

[2] It is impossible to decide whether the 'Man of Lies' is identical with the
'Preacher of Lies' who according to the Micah commentary 'misled the simple'.
This is amplified in the Habakkuk commentary (x, 9 f.) where we are told
that the Preacher of Lies incited his followers to build a city in vanity and to
establish a community in deceit, teaching false practices and scoffing at God's
chosen. (The same episode is presumably referred to in more general terms in
the Damascus Covenant, viii, 13). It is natural to see in this an allusion to a
dissident leader, who apparently set up a rival (also monastic?) community,
perhaps also in the Qumran neighbourhood: a likely enough development in

only occasion when we know that Men of War went forth from the Masadah-Qumran area with a dissident leader. We thus have some grounds for identifying, though only very tentatively, the Man of Lies with Simon bar Giora.[1]

The circumstances here proposed suggest an answer also to one other problem connected with the discoveries at Qumran. The text has not yet been published of the Copper Scrolls (originally constituting one continuous strip) found in 1952 in Cave 3, but it is known that they comprise details of the burial-place of apparently enormous quantities of treasure, mainly it is understood in the neighbourhood of Jerusalem. An obvious difficulty that arose was that it seemed inconceivable that a monastic sect should have possessed such vast resources. Hence the suggestion has been made that the whole record is fictitious, composed and inscribed with some obscure motive and having no bearing on reality: but if so, why was it inscribed in this form, on copper? In the light of what has been suggested above, however, the information regains plausibility. For the group at Qumran were as we have seen Zealots: and in A.D. 66 the Zealots captured not only the Herodian stronghold at Masadah but also the royal palace in Jerusalem, which had become the headquarters of the Roman legionaries (*Wars*, II, xvii, 2, §408: 7, §431; 434-40; 9, §451). Hence it is likely enough that they had for concealment relatively vast quantities of bullion, which would have been unlikely or impossible in other circumstances. We may however go, very hesitantly, a step further even than this. According to Josephus (*Ibid.*, xx, 3, §564), as has been mentioned above in a different connection, Eleazar ben Simon managed to get into his hands in the course of the operations in the early autumn of

---

such circumstances, closely parallelled in sectarian bodies everywhere. Attention may be drawn to the dissident Zealot who promised deliverance to those who followed him into the desert, and was killed by a punitive force sent by Festus, A.D. 60-62 (*Ant.* XX, vii, 10 §188; *Wars*, II, xiii, 4, §259-60; cf. Matthew, xxiv, 24ff.): the identification is tempting. Bar Giora, with his advanced social programme, may also be considered a 'teacher' and 'preacher', notwithstanding Josephus' picture of him as a mere gangster.

[1] There is the obvious complication, that if there had been a bitter quarrel between Simon and Menahem in Jerusalem in A.D. 66, the latter would have been unlikely to seek refuge in Masadah shortly after. But the quarrel may have seemed more serious in retrospect, after the break between the two parties, than immediately after the event. One has the impression that the motivation of not a little of the Qumran literature is extraordinarily petty.

A.D. 66 'the Roman spoils, the money taken from Cestius, and a great part of the public treasure'. In due course he and his Zealot followers entrenched themselves in the Temple, where for some time they were in control. Thus presumably they would have had in their custody a great part of the sacred treasure as well. As danger approached (whether from their internal opponents, John of Gischala and his followers, or from the Romans) it would have been natural for them to conceal their treasure in some safe place, and to make a record of what they had done. To ensure indestructibility, they might well have inscribed this record on a strip of metal: but in the nature of things, this would have been carried out roughly and clumsily, as we are told is the case with the Qumran copper documents. Certain of the Temple appurtenances, and quantities of incense, would naturally have been added to the treasure, as indeed we find in the lists (an otherwise inexplicable detail). When there was no hope left in Jerusalem, what more natural than that the documents should have been sent to the Zealot centre in Masadah-Qumran?

This is hypothesis, and we must be careful not to allow ourselves to be swept away by romantic guesswork. But it may be said that nothing in this is improbable or in contradiction to the historical facts so far as they are known.[1]

VII

The demonstration that the inhabitants of the Qumran monastery in the first century of the Christian era were Zealots seems to provide a satisfactory interpretation of many problems relating not only to the history, but also to the literature of the sect.

In the first place, we have a logical explanation for the existence and the nature of the literature. The Zealots were *ex hypothesi* a proselytising body, anxious for obvious reasons to make converts,

[1] Details regarding the text of the copper scrolls have not been published, and the information given above is based on newspaper and personal reports: cf. also Allegro, *The Dead Sea Scrolls*, appendix IV, and J. T. Milik in *The Biblical Archaeologist*, xix, 60–4. One of the places specified in the record is 'the Tomb of Zadok' near which was buried, in addition to two vessels of incense, also a duplicate copy of the schedule of concealed treasure. Possibly the individual in question was not the High Priest but the co-founder of the Zealots. The Temple treasure included incense: *Wars*, VI, viii, 3,390.

and to spread their doctrines to any region where embarrassment might be caused to the Romans. For this purpose, they made use not only of emissaries but also of the written word. Hence (if the archaeological interpretation is correct) they maintained at Qumran a scriptorium for copying their literature, which continued to operate even after the military centre had been transferred to Masadah. The nature of the literature found in the Caves seems to establish the point. In addition to Biblical works—largely the prophetical books containing promises of Redemption—there were messianic florilegia, and various apocalyptic works which further developed the same topic. Moreover, there were several copies (though fragments only survive) of the original Hebrew of the Book of Jubilees, which mystically elaborated the sect's religious calendar.

Coming now to works hitherto unknown, there are traces of eleven manuscripts of the Manual of Discipline, obviously needed as a guide for the organization of other Zealot centres that might be set up; five copies of the 'War of the Sons of Light and the Sons of Darkness', also important both for organization and inspiration; and (most suggestive in the present connection) eleven or twelve (fragmentary) copies of what was formerly termed the Zadokite (or Damascus) Document, hitherto known only from versions of a very much later date found in the Cairo Genizah. In view of this, it became obvious as mentioned above that this work emanated from the same group as that which produced the Dead Sea literature. We are now therefore in a position to affirm, quite definitely (what was formerly indeed conjectured)[1] that the 'Zadokite Document' was a product of the Zealot sect or party: more than this, it appears to have been their fundamental document, reflecting the circumstances of their establishment and their basic creed. For local use, one or two copies would surely have sufficed. That so many more were found in the Caves confirms the idea that some were written for export, for propaganda or for organizational purposes. This would explain, what has hitherto been something of a mystery, why copies should have been preserved in Egypt. We know from Josephus (*Wars*, VII, x, 1, §409 ff.) that the Zealots extended their missionary activities to that country, where as well as in Cyrene (*ibid.*, xi, 1, §437 ff.) they succeeded in organizing a dan-

[1] Cf. M. J. Lagrange, *La secte juive de la nouvelle alliance*, in R.B., xxi, 212–40, 321–60.

gerous though obviously hopeless rebellion in A.D. 73—a forerunner of the far more menacing revolt of 114/5-7, which might have been a last achievement of Zealot preaching.[1] This amply explains the preservation in Egypt of this fundamental Zealot charter, which continued to be studied and copied (perhaps in the end only as a literary curiosity) long after.[2] In view of the nature of this work, with its social and political programme, it would be natural for changes and additions to be introduced in it from time to time, reflecting contemporary conditions and requirements. This may conceivably be the reason for the fact that two different recensions were found in the Genizah, others being reflected in the fragments from Qumran.

Re-examined in the light of this hypothesis, these documents seem to contain clear but hitherto unappreciated allusions to the circumstances of the time, and to the purpose and organization for which they were written. The very first of the disciplinary regulations apparently prescribes that any person who proceeded against another Jew in a Gentile court should be put to death (ix, 1): this goes back to the interpretation suggested by the original editor, later discarded. Later (xii, 46) there seems to be an injunction that if a *sicarius* was despatched on a homicidal mission, he must not derive profit from it or remove any property with him. If we are right in postulating that the terms of the Damascus Covenant and documents were rewritten and modified according to circumstances: Text B seems to suggest (in the additions to vii, 20 and 21) that internal strife had begun among the Jewish people, reflecting the conditions of the period after A.D. 66, when the Zealots of Masadah had definitely broken with the revolutionary government in Jerusalem. A more specific allusion to the circumstances of the War agains the Romans and the siege of Jerusalem may perhaps be found in the reference in Text B (xx, 22: the corresponding passage of Text A is missing) to the 'House of Peleg who went forth from the Holy City and put their trust in God, in the epoch when Israel sinned', which could well apply to the followers of the Zealot body on the shores of the Dead Sea who held themselves aloof from the defenders of the Holy City (cf. for the significance of the name Gen. x, 25:

[1] See infra, pp. 52, 69.
[2] It is conceivable that the Genizah copies of the work in question were made at some time of crisis at the begining of the Moslem period, when circumstances again made the 'End of Days' to appear imminent.

'Peleg . . . for in his day the earth was divided' [*plg*]). It is Text B moreover which has the apparent reference to Simon bar Giora as the 'Man of Lies' and his withdrawal from Masadah in 68.

Much of the other literature found in the Caves similarly seems to bear clear indications of the circumstances in, and the group for, which they were written. This is the case even with the Thanksgiving Psalms. These, though laboriously based on Biblical models, refer throughout to the dangers and difficulties of the period (*e.g.* ii, 20–30) and more specifically to the mysteries of the right reckoning of time (i, 24: this clearly marks it as a Qumran-Zealot composition)[1] and to the Makers of Smooth Interpretations (ii, 32) who as we have seen are apparently identical with the Pharisees.[2] There is no indication here that the End of Days was considered imminent, and it is probable that these compositions (though not necessarily the extant copies) belong to a somewhat earlier period than the rest. This hypothesis is confirmed by the author's reiterated references to his discovery of the true doctrine, notwithstanding contempt and attack (iv, 8–9), to his personal escapes from his persecutors, including the Makers of Smooth Interpretations (ii, 20-3, 31-6) and to his banishment from his native country (iv, 8–9)—conceivably an allusion to the period of exile in Damascus between approximately 4 B.C. and A.D. 6, the circumstances of which have been suggested above. The most impressive evidence however is in those passages in which the author describes his place of exile, in terms which hardly admit more than one explanation: 'I praise [Thee O Lord]: for Thou hast put me at a source of flowing streams in a dry land, and (at) a spring of water in a parched land, (by) channels watering a garden of . . . a plantation of cedar and pine together with cypress for Thy glory, trees of life by a fountain of mystery, hidden amid trees lapping water' (viii, 4-6). This, as Professor Driver suggests, can only be Damascus itself, described by one living in the city as it has so often been sung by poets, where 'the chief gardens spread beneath walnuts and poplars, and the water rushed by them, swift and cold'.[3] All this goes to suggest that the author of the Thanksgiving Psalms was not the Teacher of Righteousness himself (as was suggested by Sukenik, the original

---

[1] For this point see *infra* pp. 57–9. [2] Above, p. 41.

[3] G. A. Smith, *Historical Geography of the Holy Land* (1931), pp. 674–6. There seems to be a later reference in somewhat similar terms in these Psalms, x, 25 ff.

editor) but Judah the Galilaean, the founder of the sect, whose experiences they vividly depict.

The Manual of Discipline on the other hand presumably belongs to the period after the Sectaries had established themselves at Qumran and organized their community there. It is conceivable that the constitution of the Sicarii, who are to be specifically identified with the Masadah group, as Josephus shows in several passages (e.g. *Wars*, IV, iv, 7, §399) may be referred to in cryptic terms at one point, where implicit obedience to authority, in order to avenge the Divine cause, is apparently inculcated (ix, 23–4: 'That every man should be zealous for the Statute and for its time, for the Day of Vengeance, to execute the Will in all errands of the hands and in every rule, as he is commanded'. It is noteworthy that the term מקנא is specifically used). The repeated and pointed references here to the divisions among the opponents of the sect may conceivably reflect the Jewish faction-fights in 66–70.

Another of the literary compositions found at Qumran is the so-called 'War of the Sons of Light and Sons of Darkness' (of which the almost complete text was among the original discoveries in the first cave, while four fragmentary copies were later found in the fourth cave). This goes into fantastic detail regarding the Messianic campaigns against the Kittim and their allies.[1] Ranged against them will be apparently (i, 2) the 'exiles of the wilderness' drawn from the children of Levi, Judah and Benjamin, this being a faithful enough characterization of the Zealot groups on the shore of the Dead Sea. There is no need here to go into the details of this remarkable composition, but it may be repeated that nothing in it is incongruous if we consider that it emanated from this group of *exaltés*, at the period of the Revolt against the Romans. It has been pointed out how even the equipment and strategy described can hardly be anterior to this period: that the military organization which Josephus claimed to have first introduced to the Jews while he was commanding in Galilee a year or so before is faithfully reflected; and that much attention is paid to trumpet signals which also he claims as a recent personal innovation.[1] At the beginning of the 'War of the Sons of Light and Sons of Darkness' (i, 10) we are informed that in the great army which will be assembled to fight against the latter, will be

[1] See Y. Yadin, *War*, pp. 107–130: G. Molin in Journal of Semitic Studies, i (1956) 337: K. G. Kuhn in Th.L.Z., lxxxi 30–4.

'a gathering of rams'; and in the next line the description of the battle speaks of the tumult that will be created by the 'voice of a great multitude and the trumpeting of the rams'. It is natural to interpret this as a reference to the battering-rams (Greek κριός, Latin *aries*) which played so great a part in the Roman siege-operations before Jerusalem and thus became unhappily familiar to the Jews:[1] the 'trumpeting of the rams' is a bold but graphic figure to describe the din caused by their operation. Later in the same work (v, 12–4) is a description of the weapons which would be carried by the victorious hosts of the Sons of Light, including a short sword (כדון) 'the length whereof is a cubit and a half and the breadth four fingers and the belly thereof four thumbs, and it shall be four handsbreadths to the belly; . . . and the handle of the sword shall be a true curve, cunningly wrought like embroidery in gold and silver and precious stones'. The 'belly' implies a curved blade, as Professor Driver argues, such as in fact the Romans did not know until the Imperial period (yet another proof of the relatively late date of this composition).[2] Attention has been called already in this connection to the analogy with the weapon called the *sica*. But it was a weapon similar to the Roman *sica*, which could be concealed beneath their garments, which gave not only the name but even the raison d'être to the extremist group of the Zealots, the *sicarii*: 'They used poignards of about the same length as the swords of the Persians, but curved like what the Romans term *sicae*', as Josephus informs us (*Ant.* XX, viii, 10, §186). It is surely significant that this characteristic weapon of the Zealot extremists receives in the Qumran document such detailed and even affectionate description, and was to be so lavishly and expensively adorned. The work we are discussing, the 'War of the Sons of Light and Sons of Darkness', enters into the most minute details even of the pious inscriptions that were to be inscribed on the banners of the Jewish hosts. It is an extraordinary admixture of reality, military awareness, and apocalyptic expectation. It is not very difficult to imagine Eleazar ben Jair, or one of his close associates, composing this work while he was awaiting the Divine call to go forth to battle. This too then fits admirably within the setting that we have proposed.[3]

[1] See the graphic descriptions in Josephus, *Wars*, V, vi, 4, §275 ff.

[2] The point is convincingly developed by Prof. Driver.

[3] It is noteworthy that in quoting Balaam's prophecy of the doom of the Gentiles (Numbers xxiv, 17–19), this work entirely omits the commination

In the light of all that has been said above, it would seem that throughout the period we are considering—down to the time of the destruction of Jerusalem in A.D. 70, and perhaps down almost to the fall of Masadah in A.D. 73—the sectaries remained in Qumran, continuing to copy their literature, composing new works and modifying the old in the light of the contemporary happenings, which in their eyes confirmed the exactness of prophecy and made their own final victory the more rather than the less certain. It appears that the flocks of goats in the region could have provided the material for the skins used in preparing the parchment for the documents; and perhaps devotees elsewhere brought their offerings from time to time, making it possible for the monastic scriptorium to continue its activity.[1]

The conquest of Masadah and its dependent territory by the Romans in 73 is not quite the end of the story. Some of the Zealots now escaped to Egypt, apparently bringing with them the basic literature of the sect: as suggested above, this explains the fact that the Damascus Covenant was known and copied in that country as late perhaps as the tenth century. The refugees moreover did not give up hope. So long as they maintained their faith, the Divine intervention and their enemies' overthrow were still possible. Hence, immediately after the fall of Masadah, notwithstanding the determined opposition of the local Jewish communal council, a Zealot revolt took place in Egypt, later spreading to Cyrene (*Wars*, VII, x, 1, §407 ff.). Even after its suppression, the spirit of the Zealots lived on.

Reference has been made above to the period of about Forty Years after the death of the Teacher of the Sect (conceivably

---

against the Edomites; the phrase 'Seir also, even his enemies, shall be a possession' does not figure at all, while 'Edom (אדום) shall be a possession' is changed to 'The enemy (אויב) shall be a possession' (col: II, 1. 7: cf. Yadin's edition, pp. 322–3). Such an alteration would have been strange before the conversion of the Edomites to Judaism at the close of the second century B.C.; it would have been unthinkable in the reign of the hated Edomite, Herod; it would have been natural during the War of 66–73, when the 'Idumaeans' were summoned by the Jerusalem Zealots to the capital to assist them against the priestly junta. (*Wars*, IV, iv.)

[1] Josephus emphasizes the extremely ample stores of every sort found at Masadah and their remarkable state of preservation (*Wars*, VII, viii, 4, §§295–9). Seeing that it was a royal residence and administrative centre originally, there is no reason why these should not have included prepared parchment and writing materials.

Eleazar, not his predecessor Menahem) during which those men of war who went with the Man of Lies were to pass away. This span of time seems to have played an important part in the ideology of Qumran. The *pešer* on Ps. xxxvii asserts that in a period of forty years all the wicked would have passed away, the final deliverance being possible henceforth. Clearly, this conception is patterned on the Forty Years in the Wilderness after the Exodus from Egypt (the prototype of the Redemption that was now imminent), when in a similar space of time the rebellious adults who had come forth from Egypt perished, and a purified generation emerged worthy to enter into the Holy Land.[1] It is possible that this was a later introduction into the Qumran eschatology: when it was seen that the Redemption had not come about when it was so confidently expected, justification was sought for a later date. This computation may have been responsible in part for the wave of revolt of Jewish extremists throughout the Eastern Mediterranean, in Cyrene, Egypt, Mesopotamia, Cyprus during A.D. 114/5–117—that is, about 40 years after the fall of Masadah: the spontaneity and co-ordination of these risings otherwise presents a problem that has not hitherto been explained.[2] The revolt was however savagely suppressed. Only Palestine remained quiet—perhaps through the influence of the orthodox and quietistic elements who were now in control there among the Jewish population. But, when in A.D. 132 the spirit of the Zealots again prevailed among the followers of Bar Kochba, it was natural that their former centre at Qumran should be occupied once again.[3]

[1] Cf. Joshua v, 6 and especially Ps. xcv, 10–11. The period of forty years of trial, which must obviously be correlated with Ezekiel iv, 6, similarly assumed importance in the 17th century when the Messianic movement associated with the name of Sabbetai Zevi encountered difficulties. It may be significant that this reference to the Forty Years occurs in Text B of the Damascus Covenant, which as has been suggested above seems to represent a later recension, and is extant in its present form only in a copy made at a relatively late date in Egypt. This detail might therefore have been added, after A.D. 73, in that country.

[2] For the revolt in Egypt see V. Tscherikover, *The Jews in Egypt in the Hellenistic-Roman Age* (Hebrew, with English synopsis) chapter vi, and A. Fuks in Aegyptus, xxxiii, 131–156; for Cyrene, S. Applebaum in *Zion* (Hebrew) xix, 23–56: cf. also J. Juster, *Les juifs dans l'empire romain*, ii, 185–190: K. Friedmann, *La grande ribellione giudaica sotto Traiano* in *Giornale della società asiatica Italiana*, n.s. II, 108–124: Dio Cassius, *Hist. Rom. Epit.* LXVII, xxxii, 1–3.

[3] The archaeologists' assertion, that the Qumran monastery was abandoned

VIII

It is not easy to decide definitely to what period the Qumran Sect traced its origin. According to the opening passage of the Damascus Document, it began its existence 390 years after 'Nebuchadnezzar king of Babylon'. The period is obviously based on the Bible (Ezekiel iv, 5), and probably is not to be interpreted precisely.[1] Nevertheless, 390 years after the time of the capture of Jerusalem by the Babylonians in 586 B.C. brings us to 196 B.C.—approximately the date of the definitive occupation of Judaea by the Seleucids, after the Battle of Paneas in 198 B.C.: the additional 20 years of 'uncertainty' which our source mentions comes down to 176 B.C., more or less the date of the abolition of the legitimist Zadokite High Priestly dynasty, which led up to the Hasmonaean revolt. This would hence provide a satisfactory chronological basis but for one thing: that the source asserts in uncompromising terms that the Jews lived during this 390-year period (even under the pious priestly house of Zadok, therefore!) in a parlous state, spiritually and politically, God leaving only a small remnant of them, though He refrained from giving them up to destruction. In other words, the literal interpretation of this passage would imply the utter negation of the Return from Exile and the 'ideal' period that followed it. It seems therefore that the name 'Nebuchadnezzar king of Babylon' is here used as is normal in these documents typologically, referring to the Graeco-Seleucid régime, which embraced also Babylonia. There is no reason to anticipate precise historical data or accurate reckoning of time (the later Rabbis were wildly erroneous in their estimates of the lengths of the Persian and Greek periods

---

and the cave deposit therefore ended during the war against the Romans, is here accepted. Professor Driver argues that even though the data are correct there may have been later deposits. It may be suggested that, these caves being remembered as the former Zealot manuscript-depository, cognate literature might have been brought thither later on, for concealment or for deposit, by persons associated with the sect. The question is however irrelevant to the present argument.

[1] It may be noted that this 390-year period together with the 40 years' interval during which the 'men of war' would perish (see above) comes to 430—the length of the Egyptian bondage according to Exodus xii, 37. I. Rabinowitz (J.B.L. lxxiii, II–35: cf. N. Walker, *ibid.*, lxxvi, 57–8) suggests that the 390-year period is to be reckoned not from, but up to, Nebuchadnezzar!

of domination).[1] However, 390 years from the conquests of Alexander the Great and the foundation of the Seleucid Empire would bring us to the period A.D. 57–78—not long after the foundation of the Zealot sect, and approximately the period when Menahem succeeded to the leadership.[2]

That Menahem or his nephew was the 'Teacher' of the Zealot sect has been firmly established. The suggestion has been made however that the Sect may have had more than one such Teacher in successive generations, so that all the references in the literature do not necessarily denote the same person.[3] As already mentioned, Menahem's father, Judah the Galilaean, the founder of the sect, is also described by Josephus (*Wars*, II, viii, I, §118) as a 'sophist'—even an 'outstanding sophist' (*Ibid.*, xvii, 8, §433). Possibly, the Brotherhood was at the beginning at least called by his name, if we are to interpret quite literally such expressions as 'All those who do the Law in the House of Judah' (Hab. Com. viii, i) or 'There shall be no uniting again with the House of Judah' (Damascus Covenant iv, 11). That his father, Hezekiah, and his two sons Jacob and Simon, are also to be reckoned as Teachers, is doubtful, though by no means impossible. But it is not to be doubted that the title was applied to Menahem's successor, Eleazar ben Jair; indeed, Josephus too seems to have considered him to some extent as a religious leader, to judge from the report of the dying speech (*Wars*, VII, viii, 6, §§323–6; 7, §§342–388), in which he is made to speak of himself and his followers as having been the instructors of the rest of their people. Either he or else Menahem was, then, the Teacher of Righteousness, *par excellence*. He apparently was responsible for one important innovation in the religious life of the sect: that of interpreting the Biblical prophecies as archetypes of the End of Days now imminent, thus initiating the *pešer* literature. It was the Teacher of Righteousness who led the people in the way to God's heart, making known to the later generations what

---

[1] The Rabbinical chronology as reflected in the *Seder Olam* etc. reduced the Persian period to a mere 34 years.

[2] Notwithstanding the chronological confusions indicated above, the beginning of the period of Greek domination had a definite significance in Jewish life, as the Seleucid era (beginning 312 B.C.) continued to be widely used as the 'Reckoning for Legal Deeds' (מנין שטרות) until late in, and in some countries even after, the Middle Ages.

[3] Cf. W. H. Brownlee in Bulletin of American Societies of Oriental Research, April 1952, pp. 10–20, supporting Dupont-Sommer.

He would do to the last generation (Damascus Covenant i, 10–2).
He 'teaches the Torah to his Counsel and to all who voluntarily
join him to add themselves to the chosen . . . in the counsel of
the Brotherhood, who will be saved in the day of Judgement'
(Micah Commentary, i, 5–7). It was he in whose heart God had
put wisdom 'to explain' (לפשור) all the words of his servants
the prophets, by whose hand God had recounted all that was to
happen to His people and His land in the last generation' (Habakkuk Commentary ii, 8–10);[1] and he is brought specifically
into association with the injunction to Habakkuk (ii, 2) to 'write
the vision and make it plain upon tablets, that he may run that
readeth it', which is applied in the Commentary (iv, 4–5) to
'the Teacher of Righteousness to whom God made known all
the secrets of His servants the prophets' (Ib. vii, 4–6). This
method of the Teacher was taken over and elaborated after his
death presumably by his kinsman Eleazar ben Jair. Indeed, it
seems possible to state with some confidence that the latter was
actually the author, and perhaps even the scribe, of the Commentary on Habakkuk, and not improbably of some of the similar
compositions of which fragments have survived.

There are some evidences that the Teacher of Righteousness
was himself a Priest. In the Commentary on Habakkuk (ii, 7–8)
we are told that it was the Priest 'in who[se heart] God gave
[wisdom] to explain all the words of His servants the prophets':
the Commentary on Psalm xxxvii speaks explicitly in an
otherwise mutilated passage of 'the Priest Teacher of [Righ-
teousness]'.[2] To counterbalance this however there are very
numerous instances where the Teacher is not spoken of as a priest.
It is therefore possible that the description implies not a *kohēn*
descended from Aaron, who served in the Temple, but merely
as it were a Minister of God. Taking the phrase literally, on the
other hand, we would have to decide that Menahem (as well as
his father and grandfather and presumably his successor) were
themselves priests.[3] Josephus indeed does not describe them as

---

[1] See however the next note.

[2] It is to be noted that the Habakkuk *pešer* speaks only of a Priest and his
function as interpreter, while in the Psalms *pešer* the word 'of righteousness'
is completed hypothetically (מורה ה[צדק]), the original possibly being 'the
Teacher of the Brotherhood' (מורה ה[יחד]) as in the Damascus Covenant.
Some element of uncertainty thus remains, in any case.

[3] It must however be observed here that the more one studies the Dead
Sea literature the more one is impressed by the apparent precision of the

such, but he applies the title apparently only to those associated directly with the service of the Temple.[1] If the Teacher was in fact a priest, he certainly must have claimed descent from the 'legitimist' house of Zadok, which plays so significant a part in the literature and doctrine of Qumran.[2] Conceivably therefore he considered himself to be the Priest-Redeemer ('Messiah of Judah and Aaron') designated by God.[3] The exposition of Gen. xlix. 10 seems to suggest that the sceptre had now left the tribe of Judah, with which it was to remain only so long as the institution of kingship existed,[4] thus laying open the way for the concept of the Aaronic Messiah.

---

allusions. It is possible therefore that the Priest 'in whose heart God gave wisdom to explain all the words of His servants the prophets' was not Menahem but refers solely to his successor Eleazar ben Jair, who developed his teachings and the *pešer* method. The latter (Menahem's 'kinsman' according to Josephus *Wars*, II, xvii, 9, §447: προσήκων ... κατὰ γένος) might therefore have been related to him only in the female line. In that case, the historical reconstruction given below would have to be revised, Menahem trying to dominate the Temple cultus through his kinsman, not in person. So far as the memory of Eleazar ben Jair, the defender of Masadah, survived in Jewish lore, in the pseudo-history of 'Josippon' (Joseph ben Gorion), it was as 'Eleazar the Priest'.

[1] Cf. *Wars*, II, xx, 4, §568, where he mentions his own name obliquely without the title.

[2] Normally however names are used in the Qumran literature typologically. The term 'Sons of Zadok' may therefore refer in these documents to right-thinking and right-practising priests, who 'kept the charge of My sanctuary when the children of Israel went astray' (Ezekiel xliv, 15: cf. xlviii, II): indeed this seems to be definitely implied by the Damascus Covenant (iii, 21–iv, 1). Thus all priests adhering to the Sect were *ipso facto* 'Children of Zadok'. Conceivably, the same conception might have led the dominating section in the Jerusalem Priesthood to assume the name *Zadokim* = Sadducees. (See above, page 45, note). This would explain the fact that two opposing Jewish factions were both able to associate their origins with the same name; and also that the usurping Hasmonaean house, who cannot possibly have been descended from the Zadokite line, were able to adhere ultimately to the Sadducee party.

[3] Cf. W. S. LaSor, *The Messiahs of Aaron and of Israel*, in V.T. vi, 425 ff. The language of our sources is not wholly consistent, but a single Redeemer (imminent, not eschatological) seems to be envisaged. It is conceivable that the plural is an error for the singular form, or that the documents represent different doctrines or stages of the doctrine.

[4] See N. Wieder in J.J.S., vii, 72–4, for an explanation of the passage (published by Allegro in J.B.L., lxxv, 174–5). It is interesting to note that mediaeval Jewish exegetes, such as Nahmanides, interpreted the passage somewhat in the same sense.

IX

The hypothesis that Menahem was a priest renders possible a re-examination and reinterpretation of the two convergent passages bearing on his appearance in the Temple and subsequent assassination in the autumn of A.D. 66, with which our enquiry began. As a preliminary, it is necessary to call attention once again to what seems to have been one of the fundamental tenets of the Zealots at Qumran—the religious and doctrinal importance of their own religious calendar.

As has been pointed out above, fragments of at least five different copies of the original Hebrew text of the Book of Jubilees, hitherto lost, have been discovered at Qumran. It is clear therefore that this curious work played some part in the ideology of the sect, and perhaps even derived from the same circles. The book in question (formerly ascribed to the second half of the second century B.C.), adheres on the whole (like the literature from Qumran as a whole) to the Pharisaic theology and *halakha*, although (again like the literature from Qumran) in some respects adopting more stringent standards. It drastically departs however from the Pharisaic tradition in its fixing of the religious calendar. According to its injunctions (cf. xv, 1, xliv, 4–5) the Feast of Weeks was apparently celebrated on the fifteenth instead of the sixth day of the month of Sivan. Acute analysis suggests even greater disparities—that the year always began on a Wednesday, and that it consisted of twelve months of thirty days each, with one day intercalated for each of the seasons.[1] Whether these details are precisely accurate is unimportant for our purpose. The fact of a considerable divergence for some of the major celebrations of the Jewish religious year is certain, and indeed may be referred to in the Rabbinic literature.[2]

---

[1] A. Jaubert, *Le calendrier des Jubiles et la secte de Qumran*, in V.T., iii, pp. 250–264: *Le calendrier des Jubilés et les jours liturgiques de la semaine*, ibid., vii, pp. 35–61: J. Morgenstern, *The Calendar of the Book of Jubilees: its origin and its character*, ibid., v, 34–76. The reconstructions are to some extent hypothetical, but what is clear is that the Jubilees calendar differed drastically from the accepted one.

[2] Talmudic allusions to the attempts of 'Sectaries' (*minim*) to disturb the rhythm of the Temple cultus are normally referred to the Sadducees, who however differed on principle only as regards the date of the celebration of

Whether the Qumran sect exactly followed the religious calendar of the Book of Jubilees is from our point of view immaterial, although this was probably the case. What is certain however is that they did have their religious calendar, which differed drastically from that observed by the majority of Jews. Indeed, according to the Damascus Covenant, the foundation of the sect was due principally to the realisation by the founders of this cardinal error in Jewish observance, as it had hitherto prevailed.[1]

The Book of Jubilees ends with an enthusiastic allusion to the 'seasons, and the laws of the seasons, according to the division of their days'. The Damascus Covenant speaks (iii. 12 ff.) of the remnant who held fast to the Divine covenant, and to whom were revealed the hidden things concerning which Israel had gone astray—God's holy Sabbaths and His glorious appointed times of religious observance. The Manual of Discipline (i. 13–5) gives as part of the basic rule of the sect and primary condition of membership 'not to anticipate their Times nor to be tardy in all their sacred Seasons', while the remarkable hymn at the end of the work (x, 4–5) cryptically speaks of 'the sign . . . for the opening of God's everlasting love, for the beginnings of the Seasons at every time . . . at the beginning of the months in their Seasons, and the Holy Days according to their proper observance, for remembrance in their Seasons' and so on. The Thanksgiving Psalms too (xii, 8) praise the name of God in connection with 'the basis of the Time and the period of the Sacred Seasons'. To Moses himself was ascribed a warning prophecy regarding the future time when the people would not only worship idols but also 'transgress the solemn holy assemblies and the Sabbath of Covenant and the sacred Seasons'.[2] Enough has been quoted to make it clear that the meticulous observance of a 'reformed' religious calendar was an obsession (it was hardly less) of the sect which produced the Scrolls.[3]

Pentecost (for them a movable feast, always falling on a Sunday). But those who followed the Jubilees (and Zealot) calendar obviously diverged more drastically and more frequently from the established usage.

[1] See i, 8–9, comparing with ii, 9–10.

[2] *Discoveries in the Judaean Desert*, i, 92–3.

[3] Dr. S. Talmon announced at the 1957 Conference of the Israel Society for Bible Research that an unpublished Qumran scroll makes it certain that the Sect used a solar instead of a lunar calendar. [His paper is now published in *Aspects of the Dead Sea Scrolls*, ed. C. Rabin and Y. Yadin, 1958.]

Above all, the members of the sect were concerned with the proper celebration of the Day of Atonement, 'The Fast' or 'The Time of The Fast' in their writings. The reason for this seems to be obvious. If any other religious holyday or prescribed observance was neglected, the sin was venal, and atonement could be made by repentance and the observance of the proper formalities. If however the Day of Atonement itself was not duly observed at the proper time, as God prescribed, then the people's sins remained unatoned from year to year, with a cumulative load of guilt. The argument was logical. For, since 'on this day' God accepted their atonement (Lev. xvi, 30) the ceremonies were useless if they were performed on any other day; and since the promised Redemption from Gentile oppression could come only when the people were free from sin, it was obviously dependent on the observance of the Day of Atonement with its prescribed ritual on the correct date—that is, the date as determined in the group's religious calendar. Deliverance was in fact reserved for those who kept 'The Time of the Fast'.[1] One of the basic laws of the Sect was 'to keep the Sabbath day according to its exact rules and the appointed days and the Fast Day according to the precept of the members of the 'new covenant' in the land of Damascus'.[2]

With these points in mind, then, we may revert to the story of the assassination of Mehahem ben Judah, the Teacher of Righteousness and Zealot leader, in the early stages of the revolt against the Romans in the autumn of A.D. 66.

We have seen that this was not long after the victory on the sixth day of the month Gorpiaeus, equivalent to the period

[1] Commentary on Psalm xxxvii, 9: 'Its interpretation concerns the lowly who accept the Time of the Fast and are to be saved from every trap.'

The bones of animals have been discovered at Qumran, carefully buried, and this has prompted the suggestion that possibly the sectaries there offered animal sacrifices. This would be understandable (however unorthodox) if they considered the prescribed ritual to be performed in the Temple of Jerusalem on the wrong days. Local sacrifices may be envisaged in the Discipline Manual, ix, 3–5: cf. J. Carmignac, *Les sacrifices sanglants à Qumran*, in R.B. lxiii, 524–532.

[2] Damascus Covenant, vi, 19. The Day of Atonement being the Sabbath of Sabbaths (Lev. xvi, 31, xxiii, 32), some allusions to the proper observance of 'The Sabbath' may refer to this rather than to the weekly day of rest, although the Sectaries maintained an exacting standard of observance in this respect too. The importance attached at Qumran to the Day of Atonement is reflected in the liturgical fragments for that occasion which have been found (*Discoveries in the Judaean Desert*, i, 152–9).

August-September, and that it has been calculated that this date corresponded to 3 Tishri according to the Jewish calendar, which is precisely one week before the Day of Atonement.[1] In any case, the scene of violence in the Temple was indisputably in that season of the religious year. The exact equivalent is unimportant for our purpose, since we do not know precisely how the Pharisaic calendar and that of Qumran differed. If it is true that according to the Book of Jubilees the New Year always begins on a Wednesday, the Day of Atonement must always be a Friday, when according to modern usage it never falls: it is improbable however that this regulation applied then, and this manipulation can hardly have been the basis of the objection. Hence all that can be said is that, according to Josephus, Menahem's visit to the Temple was on a day which may well have been the Day of Atonement, according to his own or to the 'orthodox' reckoning. The commentary on Habakkuk on the other hand specifically states that the clash between the Teacher of Righteousness and the so-called Wicked Priest (i.e. Eleazar, Captain of the Temple) took place on the Day of Atonement, according to the reckoning of the one faction or the other— which is not made clear.[2] ('And at the fixed time of the season of the repose of the Day of Atonement he appeared to them, to swallow them up and to make them stumble, on the fast-day Sabbath of their repose').[3]

On the assumption that the occasion the writer had in view was not the 'orthodox' Day of Atonement, but that observed by the Zealots of Qumran, and bearing in mind the hypothesis that the Teacher was a Priest, apparently with wider ambitions, let us now re-examine Josephus' story: remembering however

[1] See above, page 12.

[2] Cf. S. Talmon, *Yom Hakkipurim in the Habakkuk Scroll*, in Biblica, xxxii, 549–63, and Dupont-Sommer in V.T. ii, 229 ff. J. Obermann, *Calendarical elements in the Dead Sea Scrolls*, in J.B.L. lxxv, 285–297, opposes the Jubilees theory, maintaining that the dispute referred to in the Habakkuk *pešer* centred on the simpler question, of an intercalated month which the Sectaries opposed. It makes little difference to the present argument. It is remarkable that in later Palestinian Jewish usage, the term 'sophist', which as we have seen was applied to Menahem, denoted a reckoner or computer, especially of the calendar: cf. Targum to I. Chr. xii, 23: 'Wise in fixing New Years and New Moons and in intercalating years and months: *sophisten* in matters that concern the beginning of the month'.

[3] 'Sabbath' is not to be taken literally, the Day of Atonement being the Sabbath of Sabbaths (see above).

at the same time that he was writing for non-Jews, and was therefore likely to gloss over Jewish religious divergences, besides wishing to present his enemies in the worst possible light.

The picture now presents itself in something like the following form: Menahem the Priest, having scored a resounding victory and established his military ascendancy, believed that the day had come for reasserting the supremacy of the legitimate Priestly house (of Zadok), at the same time imposing the Zealot calendar in respect of the most solemn day of the Jewish religious year. This would put the seal on victory, ensure Divine pardon through the observance at last of the prescribed formalities on the proper day, and thus usher in the true redemption, which had already begun so propitiously with the defeat of the enemy. On the Day of Atonement according to his own reckoning, therefore, shortly after his military triumph, he went up ostentatiously (σοβαρὸς = 'Bustling, swaggering, pompous, haughty, insolent') to the Temple, attended by his following of armed Zealots (τοὺς ζηλωτὰς ἐνόπλους ἐφελκόμενος). He is arrayed, says Josephus, in royal fashion (βασιλικῇ): we must remember that the magnificent robes worn by the High Priests on the Day of Atonement, including some of gold cloth, were regarded at this period as their insignia of office. Obviously, Menahem would have had no regard for the incumbent nominated by the oppressors or by their Herodian tools, as is shown by the assassination at this time of the (ex-) High Priest Ananias (*Wars*, II, xvii, 8, §440), unless indeed this was the motive for this savage action. By virtue of descent from Zadok, Menahem could perhaps have regarded himself as being High Priest almost by hereditary right, linking up with those who had held that office (and been simultaneously at the head of the Jewish state) from the Return from Exile down to the period before the Hasmonaean revolt. He is thus indeed the 'Messiah of Aaron and Israel' whom the Qumran literature postulates.[1] Josephus says that he went up προσκυνήσων 'to prostrate himself': it is perhaps significant that prostration in worship was a particular feature of the ritual of the Day of Atonement in the Temple.[2] But more than this may have been in question—his

---

[1] Discipline Manual, ix, 11; Damascus Covenant, vii, 21a, xx, 1, xii, 23, xiv, 19.

[2] προσκυνεῖν is not a synonym for 'to pray' or 'to perform one's devotions', as implied in the Loeb translation. It is used in the Septuagint repeatedly as the rendering of the Hebrew השתחוה. This term is applied to the regular

intention was to officiate on this great day of the Jewish year, this in itself being public manifestation of his leadership, religious and political, of the Jewish people.[1]

Inevitably, the priesthood in office would have reacted violently to this presumptuous move, which threatened not only the foundation of their religious tradition but at the same time also their established position. The people as a whole, moreover, would have been horrified by this attempt, by an unauthorised person and on the wrong occasion, to celebrate the solemn ritual in the Temple. It would not therefore have been difficult for the priesthood to enlist popular support, even against a military hero. Menahem found himself opposed; and the opposition grew into a riot. It was now therefore that, in the terms of the commentary on Habakkuk (xi, 5–9) the Wicked Priest 'pursued the Teacher of Righteousness, to swallow him up, in the anger of his rage', and that, on the Day of Atonement according to the group's reckoning, he 'appeared to them, to swallow them up and make them stumble'. In thus attacking Menahem, his opponents were not guilty of a breach of the holy day; for it was not the Day of Atonement according to their calendar. The nervous Josephus—who boasted his descent from the usurping Hasmonaean priestly line—sought refuge in the Inner Court, which suggests that the riot took place in the Outer Court, before Menahem had penetrated further. The historian informs us that the people took up stones and pelted the 'arrogant sophist', reminding us of the fate prescribed for the False Prophet (Deut. xiii, 10): this itself suggests how gravely the intrusion was regarded. Political and religious passions reinforced each other, and the riot developed into a massacre: Menahem succeeded in escaping to the Hill of Ophel, but was found there not long after and cruelly put to death. It may well be that in the eyes of the faithful the great outrage was not the assault on the Teacher of Righ-

---

daily prostrations of the Priests in the course of their administrations in the Temple (M. Tamid vi, 1, 2, 3: vii, 1, etc.) and for the solemn prostration of the entire people in the Temple court at the climax of the service on the Day of Atonement (M. Yoma vi, 2). It may not perhaps be without its significance that at this point what may be termed the Zealot creed, 'Blessed be the Name. The glory of His Kingship is for ever and ever' was ecstatically proclaimed in unison. Could the word προσκυνήσων here imply this solemnity?

[1] This is on the assumption that Menahem was a Priest. If he was not, he may have tried to enforce the celebration of the ritual by one of his priestly adherents—e.g. his nephew (see pp. 55–6 n.).

teousness but the violent disturbance of his sacerdotal activity in the Temple.

This is a possible reconstruction (no more is suggested) of the event which left so profound an impression in the literature and outlook of the Qumran sect, and may indeed be said to have had a decisive influence on the entire subsequent course of the Revolution and of the disastrous War against the Romans.

X

We are now in a position to reconstruct, at least in a tentative fashion (again, no more is proposed) the history of this remarkable sect of the Zealots, in the light of the new material so unexpectedly found in the region of their former monastic centre. A new chapter is thereby added to the history of the Jewish people in the period of the great struggle against Rome.

The members of the sect possibly traced their history back, not unreasonably, to the time of the Seleucid occupation of Palestine at the beginning of the second century B.C. It was however the age of Roman domination that gave the body its impetus. The first significant name in its history is that of Hezekiah, who led a patriotic movement in the north of the country about 47 B.C. His revolt was savagely suppressed by the young Herod, recently appointed Governor of Galilee, who summarily executed him and many of his followers and overawed the Sanhedrin when they endeavoured to protest against his high-handed methods.

Hezekiah's family and followers continued to cherish his memory. After Herod's death, his son Judah, who had been living at Gamala in Gaulanitis, raised the standard of revolt. With a considerable following, he captured Sepphoris, broke open the royal arsenals to arm his adherents, and tried to establish his control over the region. This was one of a series of revolts at this time which were put down by Varus, Legate of Syria, who captured Sepphoris and reduced the inhabitants to slavery (4 B.C.). Judah escaped with some of his more devoted followers. It seems that they took refuge outside the borders of Jewish Palestine, in Syria. Here, under Judah's leadership, they apparently organized themselves into a distinctive, highly-disciplined body, who may be termed the 'Covenanters of Damascus'. They followed in most things the prevailing Pharisaic ideology and probably most of their practices, but the following distinctive features in their creed emerge:—

1. a refusal, as a religious dogma, to recognize in whatever manner any (foreign) rule over the Jewish people, whose King was God alone;
2. stringent adherence to Jewish religious law and practice, in some respects more strictly than was laid down by Pharisaic tradition;
3. the observance of a religious calendar which was in some respects in complete variance to that followed by other Jews: with as its corollary the belief that, the Day of Atonement ritual not being observed in the Temple on the proper day, the Jewish people was suffering from an accumulated burden of unatoned sin;
4. the ultimate restoration of the Priesthood to the House of Zadok.

To these points were ultimately added:—

5. the conviction that 'the End of Days' was imminent, and even happening, and that Biblical prophecy referred to these events.
6. the conviction that the head of the sect, called by them 'The Teacher of Righteousness' (possibly a Priest of the House of Zadok) had by Divine revelation learned the precise application of the Prophecies; that this special source of inspiration continued in his house; and that the Brotherhood, thus led, and observing the Law aright, would survive the present disasters, triumph over the Roman oppressor and in due course witness the Messianic age.

The 'Covenant' embodying these principles (or at least the earlier of them) may have been committed to writing shortly after the making of the compact at Damascus, but is extant only in later versions, drawn up after the Covenanters had re-established themselves in Palestine. This took place as it seems some eight or ten years later, when they occupied an abandoned 'monastic' building at a place now called Qumran, on the north-western shore of the Dead Sea. This had formerly been occupied by some Essene or Essenic body, who had left it when it had been half-ruined by the earthquake of 31 B.C.

The composition of the sect's Manual of Discipline, the almost complete text of which has been preserved (as well as fragments of other copies) may go back to this stage in their history, though it was without doubt periodically supplemented and revised. To this period may belong too the Thanksgiving Psalms, which bear the marks of having been composed by Judah the Galilaean himself during and after his period of exile. In the course of time, the sect adopted standards of religious practise and observance more rigid than those of the Pharisees, whom therefore they seem to have despised as 'Makers of Smooth Interpretations'.

The imposition of a tribute by the procurator Coponius in A.D. 6—the payment of which entailed recognition of the heathen rule, thus contravening a cardinal point of the Covenanters' code—led Judah to rise again in revolt, but unsuccessfully: he perished, and his followers were dispersed, the most devoted no doubt retiring back to their remote centre by the Dead Sea. There was a further armed revolt, or attempt at suppression, about A.D. 46–8, when the procurator Tiberius Julius Alexander crucified two of Judah's sons, Jacob and Simon, who had presumably succeeded him at the head of the Covenanters.

The leadership was now assumed by the third son, Menahem. He seems to have been the outstanding person in the history of the sect. It is to him probably that the composition or redaction of much of their religious and disciplinary literature was due. He too was apparently responsible for the organization of the 'activist' group among the Zealots, the *sicarii*, who at this period began to execute summary judgement on the Romans and their sympathizers.

The turbulent events of A.D. 66 gave Menahem, now probably in his middle sixties, the chance for which he had so long been waiting. On learning of the disorders that had broken out in Jerusalem against the Romans, he led his followers from Qumran to the palace-fortress of Masadah, further along the coast of the Dead Sea to the south. Capturing it by a *coup de main* (it is not quite certain whether from the Roman garrison or from Jewish forces which had previously occupied it), he broke open the armoury and equipped his followers, whom he now led to Jerusalem. There his strongly disciplined and well armed contingent gave him an immediate advantage over the other partisan forces, upon which he soon established his ascendancy. He skilfully directed the siege of the royal palace, and before long received the capitulation, in the late summer of A.D. 66.

He had his enemies and rivals however among the Jews: some resenting his ambition or his political radicalism, but some objecting to his singular religious doctrines and innovations—especially in the matter of the dissident calendar of his sect. He was opposed especially by the Priestly junta, under Eleazar ben Hananiah, Captain of the Temple, who had controlled the first stage of the revolt in Jerusalem before his arrival. When on the sectarian Day of Atonement therefore Menahem appeared in state in the Temple, perhaps with the intention of officiating there in his priestly capacity, disorders broke out, sedulously fostered by Eleazar and his fellow priests. The people began to stone this false prophet, who was driven out and took refuge on the Hill of Ophel. Here shortly after he was hunted down and killed by his enemies, as were also many of his followers. Another victim of the disorders was his associate Absalom, whose followers refused to support Menahem at the moment of crisis, thereby perhaps sealing his fate.

The Covenanters now withdrew again to their fastnesses on the shores of the Dead Sea, under Menahem's kinsman (probably nephew) Eleazar ben Jair. Others of the Zealots remained in Jerusalem, continuing to defend the Holy City to the last, though perpetually in conflict with the other fighters for liberty. The Covenanters at Qumran and Masadah however kept aloof from all this. The personality of the persecuted 'Teacher of Righteousness' now assumed a predominating position in their theology: and the priestly faction in Jerusalem, who had brought about his downfall (especially Eleazar, henceforth designated 'the Wicked Priest') were considered to be the enemies of the Most High, hardly less so even than the 'Kittim'—*i.e.* the Roman armies who were preparing to reinvade the land. Only when they had been swept away, and the people had turned to perfect social justice on the one hand, to correct observance of all religious prescriptions on the other, would God return to comfort the remnant of His people and give them victory. All this seems to have been formulated—perhaps by Eleazar ben Jair himself—in the form of commentaries on all or part of various Biblical books, which were interpreted in the fashion taught by Menahem, so as to refer to recent events and to the imminent Deliverance.

While awaiting the call for action, one of the leaders of the group—again, not improbably Eleazar ben Jair himself—may have drawn up moreover that amazing half-practical, half-apocalyptic military handbook which has been given the title *The War of the Sons of Light and the Sons of Darkness*, with its extraordinary admixture of sound tactics on the one hand with pious emblems, mottoes, prescriptions, prayers and ejaculations on the other. A principal occupation of the members of the community during their period of withdrawal may well have been the copying and dissemination of their propaganda material, for which they used the modest *scriptorium*, of which remains have been found at Qumran.

While the tumultuous events of the Jewish War were taking place elsewhere in the country, the Covenanters were not merely aloof, but in some respects antagonistic. We know however that they spread out from Masadah, raiding and occupying towns and areas in the vicinity. At one stage they were joined by Simon bar Giora, a partisan hero with an extreme programme of social reform, including the emancipation of the slaves; but in due course the two factions separated, Bar Giora leading his followers to Jerusalem. In July A.D. 68 Vespasian captured Jericho and visited the Dead Sea, but the Covenanters as yet remained undisturbed. When the other branch of the Zealots who were in beleaguered Jerusalem found that their condition had grown desperate, they sent to Qumran for safe custody the copper scrolls containing a list of the captured treasure which they had buried not long before.

In the summer of A.D. 70, Jerusalem fell, and the Temple went up in flames. Instead of dashing the hopes of the Covenanters, this must have raised them to a fever-pitch, for now was obviously the time for the spiritual regeneration which would immediately induce the Divine intervention and ensure triumph over all foes. This must have been therefore the culminating point of the spiritual experience of the Covenanters, and it seems likely that some of their expectant writings were composed at this period: these specifically referred to such very recent events as the burning of the Holy City and the impious action of the legionaries in setting up their standards for worship in the Temple precincts.[1]

[1] The present writer sees no reason to doubt that the composition of works of this nature was quite compatible with the mentality and circumstances of the Zealot 'republic' on the banks of the Dead Sea down to the very last

As it happens, the Romans, exhausted by the long siege, and still engaged in mopping-up operations in the immediate neighbourhood of Jerusalem, left the region around the Dead Sea alone for some time, making it possible for the Messianic camps to continue in being and even further develop their doctrines.[1]

At last the Romans were at leisure to turn their attention to this recalcitrant pocket. Lucilius Bassus, who had come to Judaea as Legate, first reduced Herodium and later the almost-impregnable Machaerus, on the east bank of the sea, also probably a Zealot stronghold. Operations were halted by his death, but in A.D. 73 his successor, Flavius Silva, attacked Masadah: it must have been at about this period that what is now Qumran —strategically the earlier objective—was abandoned by the inhabitants, who first however placed their library in safety, piously confident that they would soon be able to return. The beleaguered fortress was defended gallantly by Eleazar ben Jair, the last of the line of Judah the Galilaean, hoping for Divine

---

stages of the Revolt against the Romans, even after the Fall of Jerusalem. There is however the alternative possibility that the *War of the Sons of Light and the Sons of Darkness* and the Commentary on Habakkuk, which specifically reflect the circumstances of the period of the War, may have been composed somewhat later, partly to justify the role which the group had played in the Revolt, partly to encourage the survivors for a final effort, by the vision of an apocalyptic victory. This would of course imply that the deposit of manuscripts in the Qumran caves took place, or continued, after the occupation of the monastery by the Romans and the fall of Masadah in A.D. 73: see pp. 62–3 n. and 82. Whether these documents were written shortly before or shortly after A.D. 70–73 makes no difference to the explanation of the historical and other allusions in the Scrolls, and little to the reconstruction of the history of the period which is here tentatively put forward.

[1] Dr. Birnbaum maintains that the handwriting of the Discipline Manual is three-quarters of a century earlier than that of the Habakkuk commentary, and that of the *War* and of the *Psalms* half a century to a century later. It is not fundamental to the present thesis to maintain that the extant copies of these works are contemporary with their composition. But since the copyists at Qumran (and indeed the works in the Library) were assembled from many areas, some of them outside Palestine, rigid comparisons of personal handwriting are even less justifiable here than they are normally. Even European palaeographists, with vast amounts of dated material available for comparison, find it difficult to date a mediaeval document with perfect confidence within a period of a generation or more, on palaeographic grounds alone: it is therefore impossible to assert a greater degree of precision in the case of these hitherto unsuspected and completely isolated scripts. Apart from other considerations an aged scribe, perhaps trained in a provincial school, may maintain archaic forms for the best part of a century.

intervention down to the end. It was on the 15th of the month Xanthicus (*i.e.* about the beginning of May, A.D. 73) that the episode ended, with the mass suicide of the defenders. Zealot activity continued nevertheless, as far afield as Egypt and Cyrene; and the literature of the sect, which firmly promised deliverance after a lapse of forty years, may have been responsible for the widespread Jewish rising in A.D. 114/5–7.

The remnants of the Zealots were absorbed in due course by the followers of normative ('Pharisaic') Judaism, to whom they were very close in many ways, especially as regards their *halakha* and religious observances (though with significant reservations). In consequence, the names of successive leaders of the sect, especially Menahem ben Judah, vaguely survived in Jewish folk-lore as ideal and even Messianic figures.[1]

The foregoing restatement of certain important aspects of Jewish history in the first century of the Christian era, leading up to and reaching its climax in the great Revolt against Rome of A.D. 66–73, is necessarily tentative, and to some extent hypothetical. The substance of this monograph will however remain unaffected by the acceptance or rejection of this or that detail. What it has set out to establish seems to be in its main lines incontrovertible:—

(i)   the Teacher of Righteousness cannot be other than Menahem ben Judah, the Zealot leader, killed in A.D. 66 by the priestly faction in Jerusalem: or else his nephew and successor Eleazar ben Jair, who shared his experience but survived;

(ii)   the 'sect' which had its centre at Qumran is thus to be identified with their followers, the Zealots;

(iii)   the role, activity, outlook and history of the Zealot party differ therefore widely from what was formerly imagined, and their history must be written anew.

---

[1] It will seem paradoxical to suggest that there seem to be echoes of the Zealot outlook in the personality of the pacifist scholar Joshua ben Hananiah. Well known is the story of his great dispute concerning the date of the Day of Atonement with the Patriarch R. Gamaliel, who compelled him to travel to see him on the solemnity according to his personal reckoning (M. Rosh haShanah, ii, 8–9). Both the dispute and the vindictiveness of the sentence are understandable if R. Joshua was maintaining the sectarian views regarding the Calendar, which have been spoken of above. Our assumption would explain moreover his remark (M. Sotah iii, 4) that the 'plague of the Pharisees' was one of the banes of the world: an astonishing viewpoint for a Pharisaic leader.

APPENDIX A

THE PERSECUTION OF THE TEACHER OF RIGHTEOUSNESS
IN THE HABAKKUK COMMENTARY

The basic text concerning the central episode in the history of the Qumran sect, the Persecution of the Teacher of Righteousness, is the passage from the Habakkuk Commentary cited above (pp. 10–1) which forms the point of departure of the present monograph. The translation of this has intentionally been left obscure in the text, the interpretation being uncertain at several points.

(i) לבלעו means, literally, 'to swallow him up': so too immediately below, where the word has the plural suffix. The normal application in the context should be afflict or destroy, and this is the general interpretation. On the other hand, some scholars suggest that it means here 'to confuse' or (e.g. Talmon in *Biblica*, xxxii, 549) 'to cause to commit a ritual transgression. [Cf. however pp. 74–5 below.]

(ii) אבית is equivalent to בבית—'in the house [of]'—in which sense this unusual form appears once or twice in the Talmudic literature (b Pes. 87a, Tos. Pes. v, 9) as well as in the newly-found Bar Kochba letter.

(iii) גלותו is difficult to interpret because of uncertainty both as to the verbal root and to the implication of the third person possessive suffix, which may refer to (i) God; (ii) the Teacher of Righteousness; or (iii) the Wicked Priest.

If the reference is to God, then the word is to be pointed גְּלוֹתוֹ and the meaning is 'The House of His Revelation' (i.e. the Temple). This might however apply also to the Teacher of Righteousness, the meaning being 'the Place (perhaps the Temple in this case, also) where he revealed himself' (or 'made himself manifest').

But the word may equally well mean 'revealing' in the sense of 'uncovering'. This could signify, as Prof. Driver suggests, 'the place where he (*sc.* the Teacher) was discovered', a reference to his being dragged into the open from his place of concealment at Ophlas: cf. *Wars*, II, xvii, 9, §448, ζωγρήσαντες εἰς τὸ φανερὸν ἐξείλκυσαν; or else it could imply 'the place where he was stripped naked and put to shame'. On the other hand, it might apply to the Wicked Priest. In this case too the reference could be to the Temple, where the Priest was considered to have been guilty of uncovering his nakedness: the sensitiveness of the Qumran sect (Discipline Manual vii, 14: cf. also Book of Jubilees iii, 31) in respect to this is noteworthy, and the phrase may be a reminiscence of Ex. xx, 21 ('Neither shalt thou go up by steps unto Mine altar, that thy nakedness be not uncovered thereon')

The Jerusalem priesthood did not perhaps fulfil the sect's exacting standards in this respect, and the Temple was therefore called, sarcastically, the place of the Priest's uncovering.

Finally, many scholars favour the punctuation גָלוּתוֹ, the meaning being 'House of his Exile'. The interpretation of גלות as Exile is however a somewhat modern (i.e. post-Diaspora) conception, and would not have been so obvious in the first century. Moreover, the noun is used in the Bible only with the connotation of the exile of an entire people (cf. Is. xx, 4, Jer. xxiv, 5, xxviii, 4, Am. i, 6, 9, Ob. i, 20 &c.). If nevertheless this is the meaning here, the reference can only be to the Teacher. That גָלוּתוֹ means simply his place of residence, outside Jerusalem, is unlikely. But it could be applied to the place where he had taken refuge. It might therefore refer to 'Ophlas' where Menahem sought shelter after the attack made on him in the Temple, and whence he was dragged to his fate.

(iv) The subject of the word הופיע is not expressed. The verb is normally used in the sense of the manifestation of a superior being (cf. Deut. xxxiii, 2) but occasionally also in late Hebrew is connected with the sinful (Ecclus. xii, 15; Damascus Covenant, text B, xx, 3, 6). In the first case the implied subject is God, or the Teacher: in the second, it is the same as the subject of the previous verb—*i.e.* the Priest—which is clearly more probable. The object of the verb in this case would refer to the Teacher and his followers; in the former, to those of the Priest.

[הופיע however corresponds to הבט in the Biblical passage on which the commentary depends, this being the blameworthy action of the villain of the passage. From this it is certain that the subject must be the Wicked Priest.]

The interpretation of the passage is thus so ambiguous that it is wiser to leave the translation equivocal. What is beyond question is that it alludes to a violent clash between the Priest and the Teacher on the Day of Atonement, according to the reckoning of the one or of the other side. Any further deduction without extraneous confirmation can be questioned. But there may be seen in the text, most readily, not only an exact parallel to Josephus' account of the assassination of Menahem, but even precise verbal similarities.

APPENDIX B

WAS THE TEACHER OF RIGHTEOUSNESS PUT TO DEATH?

As has been observed in the text, the violent death of the Teacher of Righteousness at the hands of his persecutor, the Wicked Priest, is nowhere stated in quite unambiguous terms in the Habakkuk Commentary and the kindred literature. It is deduced from the phrase, twice repeated in connection with the encounter on the Day of Atonement, 'to swallow him [them] up'. This seems to imply assassination, in accordance with normal Hebrew usage, and the interpretation was taken as axiomatic from the outset by most scholars (Dupont-Sommer, Goossens, Del Medico, Allegro &c.): from this followed the sensational attempt to see in this episode the pattern for the origins of Christianity. H. H. Rowley, considering the evidence (*The Zadokite Fragments and the Dead Sea Scrolls*, p. 34), concludes that 'the language seems to me to favour this view' [that the Teacher was put to death]. Similarly, A. Michel (*Le Maître de Justice*, p. 271) concludes that 'the violent death of the Teacher of Righteousness seems to us undeniable'. A passage in the fragmentary commentary on Psalm xxxvii subsequently discovered (see above p. 11: 'the wicked priest sent against . . . (?) to kill him'), seems to make at least the intention to assassinate certain, though unfortunately the object of the verb is missing, and the text of the Psalm seems to imply that God protected His chosen one. It must be borne in mind that our documents are all defective. Even the Habakkuk commentary, though substantially complete, has some serious lacunae. It is thus possible that the tragic climax, implied in the glosses to which reference has been made above, was stated in one of the missing passages. Moreover: if the killing of the Teacher was so well known to everyone, and was so fundamental to the sect's outlook, specific mention of it might have been considered superfluous.

On the other hand, some scholars (such as J. Coppens, G. Lambert, E. Cavaignac, G. Vermès, M. Delcor, &c.) are of the opinion that the conclusion, that the Teacher of Righteousness was put to death, is unconvincing. The weight of the evidence as well as of learned opinion seems to be against them. If however they are justified, the name of Eleazar ben Jair is to be substituted for that of his kinsman, Menahem ben Judah, in the identification proposed above. All the requirements demanded by the texts (as now interpreted) and the circumstances (which remain unchanged) are then equally well satisfied. In A.D. 66, Eleazar, a member of the same family, succeeded Menahem (his uncle?) and Judah the Galilaean (his grandfather?) as head of the Zealot sect. The last-named were both according to Josephus spiritual and intellectual leaders ('sophists'). Eleazar, their successor, was obviously from this point of view in the same category, being in the eyes of his followers, potentially at least, a 'Teacher of Righteousness'. Josephus' long accounts of his dying speeches (*Wars*, VII, viii, 6, §§320–336; 7, §§341–388) confirms this picture of him: however fictitious, we may assume that they are at least in character. We know that in A.D. 66 Eleazar went to Jerusalem with his kinsman Menahem, after the outbreak of the insurrection against Rome, and took part in the subsequent military operations there. He no less than Menahem was then involved in the episode in the Temple and the violent clash which ensued: there is even a possibility that he was nominally the central figure (see above, pp. 55–6*n*.). He no less than Menahem must have been associated with and disappointed by the House of Absalom. It is certainly true of him that the Captain of the Temple ('the Wicked Priest') 'sent against him to kill him' when the armed clash took place, perhaps 'in the house of his exile', but he escaped. Eleazar then led the remnant of the Zealot task-force back to Masadah, where he continued as leader of the sect down to A.D. 73. The conjecture has already been made above that he was responsible for some part of the Qumran literature, and conceivably this literary activity of his should be more strongly emphasized.

That the Qumran sect had more than one Teacher of Righteousness, in successive generations, has already been suggested, and may indeed be considered almost self-evident; though clearly the person involved in the clash with the Wicked Priest was looked on as the Teacher *par excellence*, and is generally referred to under this title. The objection may be raised that in the Damascus Covenant there are two references to the 'gathering' of the Teacher (viii, 35, xx, 7: xx, 14) implying that he was no longer alive, whereas we know that Eleazar survived until A.D. 73, when the Qumran sect as such came to an end. In both of these cases however the form 'the Unique Teacher' or 'Teacher of the Brotherhood' (מורה [יורה] היח(י)ד) is used, and hence these passages do not necessarily refer to the Teacher of Righteousness: the precision of language in these documents has already been noted.

To sum up: The Teacher of Righteousness of the Dead Sea literature is indubitably the head of the Zealot Party, who was persecuted by the Captain of the Temple: it is only on this assumption that the literature as a whole becomes coherent and the historical allusions in it can be consistently interpreted. From the language used, it appears that the Teacher was assassinated, in which case he is to be identified with Menahem ben Judah (died A.D. 66). If however this was not the case, then he is to be identified with Menahem's kinsman, Eleazar ben Jair (d. 73). The background, the allusions, and the central episode are the same in either case.

APPENDIX C

THE HOUSE OF ABSALOM

As has been observed above, the more one reads the text of the Dead Sea literature the more one is impressed by the precision of the language in the historical allusions. This fact justifies re-examination of the important passage in the Habakkuk Commentary (v, 8–12) of which use has been made at the beginning of this study:—

'*Wherefore do you look on, ye treacherous, and keep silence when the Wicked One swalloweth up one more righteous than himself* (Hab. i. 13, with variations). Its interpretation concerns the House of Absalom and the men of their counsel, who were silent at the time of the suffering of the Teacher of Righteousness, and did not help him against the Man of Lies, who rejected the Law in the midst of all their congregation.'

The translation here given is that imposed by the lemma, which has been overlooked to some extent by the students of these documents. Thus נדמו may mean 'cut down', but it interprets ותחריש of the text, and here therefore must have the meaning 'were silent'. Similarly, בתוכחת may mean 'through the reproof of', or 'at the time of the reproof of', but it interprets בבלע of the text, and must therefore here imply 'suffering' or 'punishment', as in II Kings xix, 3, Is. xxxvii, 3, Hosea v, 9, Ps. cxlix, 7. Notwithstanding what may have been said previously, these points do not admit of any doubt. Conversely, בבלע being used to explain בתוכחת, it can be argued that the root בלע used elsewhere in this work in connection with the Teacher of Righteousness (lit. 'to swallow up') must mean, not to confuse &c., as has been proposed, but 'to afflict' or 'to punish': this is an additional indication therefore of the violent attack on the Teacher of Righteousness by the Wicked Priest.

The use of the phrase 'the House of Absalom' seems to suggest, if the words are used precisely, that the followers of Absalom are in question, not Absalom himself. He was killed during the disorders in Jerusalem in the early autumn of A.D. 66, and Josephus' phrase τόν ἐπισημότατον τῆς τυραννίδος ὑπηρέτην (in contradistinction to τους ὑπ' αὐτον ἡγεμόνας) seems to imply that he was not a 'lieutenant' of Menahem's, on the same footing as the others, but the leader of an associated group. Josephus does not give a day-by-day account of what was happening, and he may have perished at any stage in the disorders, from the time of the initial clash in the Temple onwards. After his death, his former followers would naturally have been called 'The House of Absalom': this slightly oblique and idiomatic phrase perhaps made it easier for the author to depart from his normal rule of using names typologically.

In the Habakkuk commentary, it is stated that the House of Absalom and their associates ('the men of their counsel') stood aloof, failing to intervene at the time of tribulation for the Teacher of Righteousness, when a clash took place between him and the Man of Lies, who publicly rejected the Law. Absalom himself is no longer in evidence, this being a further argument for identifying him with the only known character of this name, of the Second Temple period, who lost his life but apparently left disciples who could be designated as 'The House of Absalom'.

If the identification is accepted of the Man of Lies with Simon bar Giora, as suggested above in the text (pp. 42-4), the following picture may now emerge:—

We know from Josephus that immediately before the Revolt, Judaea was approaching a state of anarchy, several insurgent leaders attached to the Zealots being active in various places. Among these were, in addition to Menahem ben Judah and (as I suggest) Absalom, two others of special note: Simon bar Giora and Eleazar ben Simon, who were to have an active share in all the military operations down to the fall of Jerusalem in A.D. 70. Josephus emphasizes the decisive part these two took in the operations against the Romans at the outset of the revolt of A.D. 66, and for this purpose it is certain that they must already have had organized bands of followers who acknowledged their leadership. When hostilities began, all of these groups converged on the capital, combining with but at the same time overshadowing the priestly and aristocratic elements who had hitherto taken the lead there. It was this combination of forces, under Menahem, which achieved the great triumph on 6 Gorpiaeus.

In asserting his sectarian religious views, Menahem, the leader of the pure 'monastic' Zealots who adhered to the Damascus Covenant, now counted on the support of all the various Zealot and quasi-Zealot groups. The Man of Lies, Simon bar Giora, defected, however—publicly adhering to the 'traditional' religious party, joining with the Priestly faction in order to suppress the Teacher, and thus 'rejecting the (true) law in the midst of all their congregation'. Conceivably, he headed the body who dragged Menahem out of his hiding-place at Ophlas to his death. Still however the Teacher counted on the support of the followers of the other partisan leader, Absalom, who had died at the outset of the recent disorders, and who was apparently closer to him in outlook. Nevertheless, they, 'the House of Absalom', stood aloof 'together with their associates' and were 'silent'. Thereby, as traitors (בוגדים) they earned the undying hatred of the writer of the Habakkuk commentary and of his followers. It was perhaps this unexpected defection which turned the scales against Menahem ben Judah and sealed his fate.

It is no objection against this reconstruction that so little of this is stated explicitly by Josephus, who was writing a history of the Jewish War against the Romans, from a strongly anti-Zealot point of view, and for the benefit of non-Jews who were uninterested in what they regarded as unimportant internal squabbles.[1]

---

[1] [This note, written after the volume had been handed to the publisher, expands and in certain points modifies the account given above in the text.]

APPENDIX D

THE KITTIM AND THE END OF DAYS

In the investigation of the problems connected with the Dead Sea Scrolls, sufficient attention has not been paid hitherto to the close relation between the Kittim and the End of Days. This name was not chosen arbitrarily or casually by the writers of this literature to designate their opponents, but clearly derives from Balaam's considered prophecy of 'The End of Days' (אחרית הימים) in Numbers xxiv, 14–25. The seer first refers to the triumphs which Israel 'doing valiantly' would at that time achieve over his traditional enemies: this is the basis presumably of the description of the campaigns against the neighbouring peoples at the beginning of the 'War of the Sons of Light and the Sons of Darkness'. The prophecy reaches its climax with the emphatic conclusion: 'BUT HOSTS (?) SHALL COME FROM THE COAST OF THE KITTIM, AND THEY SHALL AFFLICT ASSHUR AND THEY SHALL AFFLICT EBER (i.e. the Hebrews): AND HE ALSO SHALL COME TO DESTRUCTION'. This, if properly understood, must obviously be the fundamental prophecy of the End of Days: those in the Prophets &c. are in general euphoric terms, while that in Jacob's blessing (Genesis xlix, I) deals only with the Tribes of Israel. (It is significant that the Rabbis assert that the Patriarch now suddenly lost the spirit of prophecy so that in fact he did not describe the 'end of days' as he had promised.) In this passage of the Book of Numbers however Balaam foretells in positive terms the tribulation of the Jewish people in the 'end of days' at the hands of the Kittim, to be followed in due course by the annihilation of their persecutors: this fairly obvious interpretation is that given by all the ancient Jewish versions. Hence, what the name may originally have meant or implied is beside the point. The Kittim in the present connotation are not merely some specific people, nor yet some specific enemy people, but the *ultimate* enemy. The name is thus like other names in the Qumran literature typological, denoting (as continued to be the case in later Rabbinic exegesis) the arch-persecutors of the Jews at the time when the document or the interpretation was written, whose imminent downfall would mark the 'end of days'.

Thus, the term Kittim could conceivably have applied to the Greeks, but only at the time when they were actively persecuting the Jews of Palestine and threatening their existence: i.e. in the relatively brief period of Seleucid oppression, between say 175 B.C. and 165 B.C.[1]

---

[1] [As indeed is the case in I Maccabees i, 1 and viii, 5.]

Before 175 B.C., they were not persecutors, after 165 B.C. (or a little later) their menace in this sense was ended.

If in the Qumran literature the term Kittim implies the Seleucids or the Greeks (as some scholars stubbornly maintain), it must necessarily refer therefore to this very brief period of time. Moreover, with the end of the Seleucid domination in Palestine the conception would obviously have lost its validity, and the literature concentrating on it would have retained only academic interest. Hence it is out of the question to ascribe the historical allusions in these writings to the period of the Hasmonaean monarchy (e.g. to the reign of Alexander Jannaeus): if the Kittim are intended to imply the Greeks, we would of necessity have to look for the Teacher of Righteousness and the Wicked Priest, who figure in the same context, in the circumstances of the period of, or immediately preceding, the Hasmonaean revolt, when the Seleucids were 'afflicting Eber', i.e. threatening the existence of the Jewish people. Moreover: all the literature mentioning the Kittim and their might would also have to belong to this period or else to the halcyon theocratic days at the very beginning of Hasmonaean rule: for it soon became apparent especially to pietists that the Seleucids were not the ultimate enemy, and that their overthrow had not ushered in the End of Days. As soon as the Romans had established their oppressive authority in Palestine, these documents would have lost entirely the last shreds of their validity, for it would now have been tragically plain that the application of the 'eschatological' prophecies to the Greeks had been completely misleading.

Hence the interpretation of the term Kittim in the Qumran literature as meaning the Graeco-Seleucids would have as its corollary, not only that the basic documents were written within a few years of 165 B.C., but also that the Qumran sect ended its separate existence, with the disappearance of its theoretical basis, in or immediately after 63 B.C. This certainly was not the case.

This excursus should not have been necessary, for—quite apart from the obvious first-century references in the literature—an objective reading of the documents conveys in the clearest fashion an impression which is true of the Romans, and of no other people of antiquity with whom the Jews were in contact.[1]

---

[1] It is to be noted that Asshur figures in Balaam's prophecy as a victim of the Kittim, but in the Qumran literature as an associate. From the references at the outset of the *War of the Sons of Light and Sons of Darkness* to the campaign conducted against the Kittim of Asshur, it seems as though the text which served as the basis of the Qumran exegesis read something like וצים מיד כתים ואשור יענו עבר וגם הוא עדי אבד *Kittim* is apparently applied to the Romans in Daniel xi, 30, which seems to be a sort of elaboration of Balaam's prophecy applied to the earlier crisis. [Cf. also Ez. xxvii, 6.]

Important corollaries seem to follow from the assumption that Balaam's last words were regarded as the fundamental prophecy of deliverance. Apparently, this was originally applied to the founder of the Zealot sect. Text A of the Damascus Covenant, which it is suggested may represent its earlier version, states (vii, 18–20) that 'The Star is the expounder of the Law who comes to Damascus, as it is written: "A Star shall step out of Jacob and a sceptre shall arise out of Israel" (Numbers xxiv, 17). The Sceptre is the Prince of the whole congregation, and when he arises he shall strike down all the sons of Seth'. In text B, which represents the later recension, this passage is omitted: by now, it had become obvious that this original expounder of the Law was not the promised Star who was to come triumphantly from Jacob. But the hopes of deliverance continued to centre on this passage, which was quoted by Rabbi Akiba when he encountered Simon ben Kosiba, the leader of the revolt of 132–5 A.D. This was not a picturesque Midrash: Akiba's meaning was that Simon was the Star on whom the prophecy (cherished formerly in particular by the Zealots[1]) centred: the subsequent changing of the patriot leader's name popularly to Simon bar Kochba (=son of the Star) may in fact be considered characteristic of Qumran exegesis. The Star shown above the Temple on the Bar Kochba coins is now seen to have a remarkable pertinence. Talmon has suggested (*Biblica* xxxii, 549–563) the possibility that the dispute concerning the Calendar and in particular the observance of the Day of Atonement, when Akiba acted as mediator, may link up with the Qumran calendrical obsession. All this goes to support the possibility that Qumran-Zealot doctrine continued to be a powerful force within Pharisaic Judaism after the suppression of the great 'First Revolt' against Rome.

APPENDIX E

MENAHEM THE ZEALOT LEADER IN JEWISH LEGEND

There is curious evidence that the recollection not only of the name of Menahem (see above, p. 17*n*.) but also of the details of his career were long preserved by the Zealots and those who came after them, lingered

---

[1] This is presumably the famous prophecy which so encouraged the Jews, mentioned not only by Josephus (*Wars* VI, v, 4, §§312–3) but also by Tacitus (*Hist.* v, 13) and Suetonius (*Vespasianus*, §4), according to which one coming from Judaea would rule the entire world. Nothing more closely corresponding to it than this verse (which had remarkable prominence in the Qumran literature: see Yadin, *op. cit.*, pp. 194, 323) is to be found anywhere in the Bible.

on for many centuries, and helped to build up the messianic fantasie-current among the Jewish people in the Middle Ages. It may be that his death, notwithstanding the high hopes centred in him, was responsible for the theory of the Messiah of the Tribe of Joseph, who would appear, achieve temporary victory, die at his enemies' hands, and then be followed by the Messiah of the House of David who would achieve the final redemption. The following composite picture emerges from the various sources collected in Judah Ibn-Shemuel's compilation on legends of the Redemption (*Midrashe haGeulah*: 2nd ed., Jerusalem 1954):—

The name of the true Messiah is Menahem (ben Amiel), as mentioned in the Talmud (*Sefer Zerubbabel* p. 76): he will be preceded however by the Messiah ben Joseph, Nehemiah (a variant form of Menahem) ben Hushiel: the latter is however called Menahem in at least one source (Hymn by Kalir, p. 107). Nehemiah-Menahem will begin his career by heading a successful rising against the oppressor in Upper Galilee (*Agadat haMashiah*, p. 103: *Inyane haYeshua*, p. 135). He will then go to Jerusalem, where he will defeat the Roman armies (*Pirke Mashiah*, p. 316) and offer sacrifice in the Temple. Ten monarchs will rise over the Gentiles in rapid succession, and will wage war against Jerusalem (*Sepher Zerubbabel*, p. 80). At this time, an impudent-faced King will pervert the Calendar (*Aggadat haMashiah*, p. 103). In the fighting Nehemiah-Menahem will be killed, and his body left lying in front of the city gates (*Sepher Zerubbabel*, p. 81). Hostilities will now take place in the Plain of Acco[1] (Hymn by Kalir p. 160). Great tribulation will follow for the Jews, and those who remain faithful will take refuge in the wilderness (*Agadat haMashiah*, p. 104). Then the Messiah ben David will arise and defeat the enemy, the Messiah ben Joseph being resurrected and the great Deliverance being achieved (*Sefer Zerubbabel*, p. 83).

It would take up far too much space and time to develop this theme further here, or to trace all these legends to their source and emphasize the various parallels. It must be made clear moreover that the picture that has been conveyed is based on a subjective selection from the documents in question, neglecting chronology, stressing similarities and overlooking divergences. In spite of this however the points of contact between this and the story of Menahem, as it emerges from Josephus and the Qumran literature, is extraordinarily striking. It certainly seems as though the recollection of Menahem the Zealot leader and of the doctrines of the Qumran sect lingered in folk-memory

[1] בבקעת עכו ילחמו: the text published by Allegro, J.B.L. lxxv, 178 (see above, p. 36) has בבקעת עכו ללחם, but I cannot see any other correspondence. 'The Plain of Acco' does not however seem to be a common term or to occur in the Talmudic literature, and the coincidence is noteworthy: did Kalir and the florilegium have a common source?

in a vague fashion well into the Middle Ages. The evidence strengthens our hypothesis that Menahem was not merely a military leader, and that his teaching and his end created a profound impression. The amalgamation in this composite account of some elements which conform with the story in Josephus and others which conform with the picture conveyed by the Qumran literature seems to corroborate the identification of Menahem ben Judah with the Teacher of Righteousness. It is natural to imagine that in due course the Zealots became merged in the Pharisees and that they brought with them some of the sectarian legend, which in due course became merged in the common store of Jewish folk-lore.

APPENDIX F

OPHEL IN THE QUMRAN LITERATURE

As this work was passing through the press, a new line of approach has occurred to the author which suggests a striking and specific reference in the Qumran literature to the events in Jerusalem in the autumn of A.D. 66. One of the outstanding Biblical prophecies concerning the End of Days is in the Book of Micah. Obviously therefore it must have been the object of apocalyptic study at Qumran, and it is in fact among the Biblical works fragments of a *pešer* on which are extant. The book applies indeed exactly to the circumstances of 66–70 as seen through Zealot eyes: it describes the tribulations of Jerusalem at the hands of a pitiless foreign enemy, the wrong-doing of its rulers, and then the final triumph of righteousness at the End of Days. This section states (iv, 8):

And thou, Tower of the Flock, Ophel of the daughter of Zion, unto thee shall he come: yea, the former dominion shall come, the kingdom of the daughter of Zion.

Whatever the precise meaning of this extremely difficult passage, it certainly seems to imply that the hill of Ophel near Jerusalem was to play an important role in the origin of the renewed Jewish state that was to arise at the End of Days: here would begin the 'dominion' that would save the people of God from their tribulation. Certainly, this point must have been emphasised in the lost part of the *pešer*— such an opportunity was too good to miss.

Now it was in Ophel (Ophlas), as we have seen above on the authority of Josephus, that the central episode in the history of the Dead Sea sect took place. There Menahem ben Judah was killed by the Wicked Priest. Thence Eleazar ben Jair led the righteous remnant to the Dead Sea area, to maintain the nucleus of the Kingdom of Saints and await the final Deliverance.

The association of this episode with the Biblical text in the eyes of Qumran seems obvious, and a reference to it presumably occurred at this point in the *pešer*. He (the Teacher of Righteousness) came to Ophel at the climax of his career: here thereafter began the anticipated final Kingdom of the Daughter of Zion.

It seems possible even that the prophet Micah's reference to Ophel may have given the impetus to this association of ideas on the part of the members of the Qumran sect, making them imagine that their history was specifically envisaged in the prophecies of the End of Days. We find Zealot experience reflected, once again, in the basic literature of the Dead Sea sect. However slight the individual importance of all these pieces of evidence, their cumulative weight is overwhelming.

APPENDIX G

WERE THE QUMRAN SECTARIES ESSENES?

When the Judaean Scrolls were first discovered, most scholars not unnaturally assumed that the members of the Qumran sect, situated on the west coast of the Dead Sea not far from Engedi, were identical with the Essenes, who, according to Pliny (but to Pliny alone, among the ancient authorities) lived near the west coast of the Dead Sea, 'above' Engedi (*Historia naturalis*, V, xvii, 73). There are weighty objections to this identification, for the doctrines and practices of the two bodies so far as they are known to us do not by any means coincide, as is shown above (pp. 22–3). But adequate attention has not been paid to the most serious difficulty arising out of Pliny's text, which taken in conjunction with later archaeological investigations make the equation quite impossible. Discoveries at Qumran since 1948 have definitely proved that the 'monastery' there was sacked and destroyed during the War of 66–73, being occupied thereafter by a Roman garrison. Pliny, on the other hand, depicts the Essenes as still living their idyllic monastic lives, far enough from the Dead Sea coast to avoid its noxious exhalations (this detail too must be taken into account) at the time when he prepared his work for publication, in or very shortly before the year 77: for he speaks in this passage precisely and consistently in the present tense (*fugiunt . . . nascitur . . . gens aeterna est*). He is clearly referring to conditions in Palestine (which he perhaps knew personally, having served there with Titus) *after* the War. That this is the case is made quite certain by the fact that two paragraphs earlier he alludes to the destruction of Jerusalem (*in qua fuere Hierosolyma*) and in the next sentence to the utter devastation of the palm-groves of Engedi as a result of the hostilities (*infra hos*

Engada oppidum fuit . . . nunc alterum bustum). His description of the Essenes, living undisturbed some distance away from the Dead Sea, must similarly therefore refer to the post-war period. With this, the evidence for associating the Essenes with Qumran entirely disappears. Whoever was in occupation of the 'monastery' there before 68, it was not the exemplary Essenes to whom Pliny refers.[1]

APPENDIX H

THE ERA OF THE HABAKKUK COMMENTARY

The eminent scholars who have set themselves to the elucidation of the problem of the Qumran sect in its historical setting have tended to decide on their solution and then accommodate the details. I propose here to reverse the process and to attempt to determine from internal evidences, very summarily, merely to what period the documents refer, leaving aside at present the solution of the precise problem. I will confine myself to the evidence provided by the Habakkuk Commentary which so far as it goes is tolerably complete, and unlike most of the other documents uses on the whole clear language, although concealing the identity of the principal characters by the use of sobriquets—no doubt fully intelligible at the time, however difficult of comprehension to us.

(i) The Commentary postulates a period which it considers the End of Days, which had already begun. The End of Days is necessarily a relatively restricted period comprised within an ordinary lifespan or generation (as explicitly indicated in ii. 7 and vii. 2[2]) before and including the final Deliverance, which was to introduce a period of perpetual felicity.

(ii) A feature of the End of Days in accordance with Biblical prophecy (Numbers, chapter xxiv) is the suffering of the Jews at the hands of a relentless military people, the Kittim (ibidem, verse 24) who had now occupied or were about to occupy Judaea. The term Kittim was applied to the invader with reference to Numbers

[1] It would be tortuous to maintain that Qumran was destroyed in the War by some over-zealous subordinate officer, notwithstanding the exemplary conduct of its inmates, who then retired to a new home somewhat further inland. But if this had happened, there would have been no reason to prevent them from continuing to use their traditional cave-depository at Qumran for their manuscripts, so that the *terminus ad quem* of 68 (or 73) for the historical allusions in these would automatically lose its validity.

[2] ii. 7: 'Who did not believe when they heard from the Priest all that is to come on the Last Generation'; vii. 2: 'And God spoke to Habakkuk to write all that is to come on the Last Generation'.

xxiv. 24, in the conviction that this was not an ordinary enemy, but the Ultimate Enemy of the Jewish people, whose overwhelming would characterise and usher in the End of Days.

(iii) In view of what has been said thus far, this people, the Kittim, can be identified only with the Greeks (before 165 B.C.), less probably the Parthians (in 40 B.C.) or else the Romans (at various periods, from about 63 B.C. onwards).

(iv) The Qumran sect remained in being as a sect as is universally agreed until the War of 66/73 (whether or no its monastic centre was captured precisely in the year 68 as many scholars maintain need not be discussed here). Up to this period its specific literature, including the Habakkuk commentary, was still current and valid. At this time therefore the sectaries still imagined that the Kittim were the Ultimate Enemy, whose invasion of Judaea marked the End of Days. But after the Hasmonaean triumph it became evident that the defeat of the Greeks had not ushered in the End of Days and the establishment of the ideal and abiding Hebrew commonwealth of prophetic vision: after 37 B.C. it was evident that the withdrawal of the Parthians had left the way open to the worst and most powerful of all oppressors. Hence, whatever the term may or may not have signified earlier, in the eyes of the sectaries established at Qumran in the first century the Kittim could not be the Greeks or the Parthians, and must be the Romans: and the historical references in the Habakkuk commentary relating to the Kittim and the End of Days must be to persons and events subsequent to the invasion of Syria by Pompey in 63 B.C.[1])

(v) The Teacher of Righteousness taught at the End of Days, at the time of the Kittim: therefore the Teacher also belongs to the Roman period (after 63 B.C.).

(vi) The Qumran sect retained its separate existence and vitality as expressed in its literature until the beginning (at least) of the War against the Romans of 66/73. At this time they therefore imagined that they were in the midst of the End of Days, for the End of Days cannot already have been enacted. The events and personalities associated with the End of Days must hence necessarily belong to approximately this period or generation.

(vii) In view of all this it is clear that the central episodes in the

[1] The Qumran literature cannot be compared of course in this respect with the Book of Daniel, which, apparently composed with reference to the Greek oppression, remained current in and after the period of Roman oppression: for the cryptic style of this work made possible reinterpretation or progressive interpretation, in a manner which the precise details of the Habakkuk Commentary (e.g. the clash between the Teacher and the Priest on the Day of Atonement) positively do not.

history of the Qumran sect, referred to in the Habakkuk Commentary, took place not many years before the destruction of the monastic centre in which they lived, during the War of 66/73: and the principal characters mentioned in this work (such as the Teacher of Righteousness and the Wicked Priest) flourished within this generation.

(viii) The Qumran literature was the literature of the Sectaries who were in occupation of the site at the time of the Roman invasion of A.D. 66/73. Yet this element first occupied the site in or very shortly before A.D. 6: to assume their identity with the occupants who abandoned the site in 31 B.C. is wholly unreasonable in the absence of confirmatory evidence. There is therefore every reason to imagine that the historical experience of the Qumran sect, as a sect, did not antedate the Christian era.

(ix) The Habakkuk Commentary is apparently incomplete, or rather unfinished, not covering the last chapter of the Biblical work, although this lent itself especially to apocalyptic interpretation. Obviously on the other hand the subject-matter of the Commentary, as of the remainder of the sectarian literature, was still valid at the time of the capture of Qumran during the War of 66/73. Hence it was still in the process of composition at this time: and the parts already composed must refer to the period of or leading up to the War. The central characters therefore belong to this generation[1]).

(x) The conclusion, that the background of the Habakkuk Commentary refers to the events of the period of Roman domination, culminating in the War of 66/73, can be reasonably disputed only on one of the following assumptions:—

a) That the End of Days extended (or was believed to extend) over a period of several generations—if the sect is pre-Maccabaean, as long as 250 years!

b) That the Teacher of Righetousness who flourished long before was to rise from the dead at the End of Days, still in the future (this providing a parallel to the basic story of Christianity).

c) That the Sect continued in vigorous existence in or near Qumran well after the War of 66/73.

d) That the Sect came to an end with the earthquake and abandonment of the Qumran monastery in 31 B.C., when the sectarian library was placed for safety in the near-by caves, the denizens

[1] This argument would be invalidated if as is remotely possible the last chapter of Habakkuk did not yet form part of the Biblical book. On the other hand, it is noteworthy that the apparent references to the War of 66/73 (e.g. the Sack of Jerusalem and the worship of the Roman standards in the Temple court) are precisely in the work which may reasonably be assumed to have been in the process of composition at this time.

after A.D. 6 having no connexion with their predecessors: the most cogent arguments for fixing the historical background in the generation culminating in A.D. 66/73 being thus applicable to the period before 31 B.C.

The first of these possibilities (a) is ruled out not only by inherent improbability but also by the fact that as mentioned the End of Days is specifically identified in the Habakkuk Commentary with a single generation; the second (b) is based on what is at the best an equivocal interpretation of the Hebrew text; the third (c) contradicts historical and archaeological evidences, but if it is entertained would imply that the solution is to be sought in the period subsequent to the War of 66/73; the last (d) is the only way in which a Maccabaean dating for the principal events is reconcilable with the evidences; but it has never been put forward even by the champions of these views because of its inherent improbability, and need not therefore be taken into serious consideration.

APPENDIX I

THE ZEALOTS—A JEWISH RELIGIOUS SECT

Josephus begins his famous description of the religious sects among the Jews in his day (*Wars of the Jews,* 11. viii: *Jewish Antiquities,* xviii. 11–22) by describing the activities of Judah the Galilaean, 'a sophist, who founded a sect of his own, having nothing in common with others'. He then goes on to give a summary account of the doctrines of the Pharisees, the Sadducees, and especially the Essenes, to whom and whose saintly way of life, he devotes several pages of almost dithyrambic praise. Regarding the 'Fourth Philosophy' of Judah the Galilaean, however, he tells us only that its followers agreed in all other things with Pharisaic ideas, except that they had an inviolable attachment to liberty, saying that God was their only Ruler and Lord. Later, he speaks of this faction, whom he refers to apparently sometimes as Zealots (the name generally applied to them now) sometimes as *Sicarii*,[1] as having been mainly responsible by reason of their intransigence for the horrors of the war against Rome and its terrible aftermath. In fact, except at the very outset he depicts the Zealots not as a religious group but rather as a party of deplorably bellicose political extremists *à outrance*. That is the picture of them that generally prevails, and some historians of the period have gone so far as to deny that they could be considered a

---

[1] I discuss this identification in an article in the Manchester *Journal of Semitic Studies* (October 1959, pp. 332–355) on the Zealots in the War of 66–73. But it is in no way fundamental to my general thesis.

'sect' in the generally accepted sense of the word. This in fact has been, whether explicitly or implicitly, one of the main arguments against the present writer's identification of the Sect of the Dead Sea Scrolls with the Zealots. The Dead Sea literature expresses the outlook and organisation of God-intoxicated visionaries: from Josephus, we have the picture of the Zealots as a coterie of bloodthirsty political gangsters. What (we are asked) can there be in common between the two?

Josephus, himself, however, much though he hated the Zealots and all their works, makes it abundantly clear that whatever their political activities, they were to be considered a religious sect in the more specific sense: that is, a body of men holding distinctive religious doctrines and (in the Jewish context) with specific religious practices. He speaks of Judah the Galilaean as having founded, in conjunction with a Pharisee named Zadok, the Fourth Philosophy, additional though analogous that is to the three existing 'philosophies' of the Sadducees, the Essenes, and the Pharisees, although in most respects (as he informs us) approximating to the last-named. Moreover, he describes the founder of the sect, Judah, and later on his son and ultimate successor in its leadership, Menahem, as being a 'sophist': in one case, an 'outstanding sophist'. The precise significance of this term in the context is not easy to determine—at that time, it did not have the contemptuous meaning that it was later to acquire. But in any case, it connotes something in the nature of 'teacher' or 'intellectual': the historian uses it elsewhere in reference to the two heroic Rabbis who maintained that Herod's placing of a Roman eagle over the Temple gate was an infringement of Jewish law, and incited their disciples to remove it. Hence it is clear that Josephus regarded the hereditary leaders of the Zealots in successive generations, not merely as military chieftains and partisan leaders, but also as teachers—in the circumstances of the time, religious teachers—however profoundly he disagreed with what they taught.

Even without this evidence, we are driven to the same conclusion if we take the circumstances of the time into consideration. For in first-century Judaea, with its universal religious intoxication extending to every segment of the population, any political attitude had to have a religious sanction. Not only the Zealots, but one imagines every other faction and faction leader who came into prominence at the time, must have claimed Divine approval for its outlook and actions, perhaps resting on the specific interpretation of certain Biblical passages. Thus, for example, it is self-evident that Simon bar Giora, the last hero of Jewish freedom at the time of the siege of Jerusalem, with his far-reaching social and economic programme, must have claimed that in freeing the slaves and liberating the debtors he too was fulfilling the Divine will, and that the Jewish people could not hope for victory until they carried this programme into effect. (He is spoken of as a Zealot by most modern historians of the period, but our only contemporary source, Josephus, specifically excludes him from this category). That his doctrines too were crystallised in written form is likely enough, if not indeed certain: and there is no inherent reason why the literature of his faction should not have been preserved also in the same manner as that of the Qumran sect. And the various 'prophets' of whose ratiocinations Josephus blandly informs us at the time of the siege of Jerusalem certainly combined in their utterances political, ethical, and social teachings and warnings, in the classical Jewish fashion. To think of the Zealots as a 'political' faction in the modern sense is therefore an obvious anachronism; even as a political party, they must necessarily have been from some points of view also a religious sect or faction.

In his account in the *Jewish Antiquities* Josephus informs us that the Zealots agreed with the Pharisees 'in all things' except for their basic political doctrine, but in the *Wars* he states that the sect founded by Judah the Galilaean 'had nothing in common with the others'. The contradiction is presumably to be reconciled by assuming that although the ideas and practices of the Zealots were similar to those of the Pharisees, and certainly nearer to them than to those of the other two sects, there were certain differences of interpretation and of outlook which made it possible to consider them an entirely separate body. The Dead Sea literature speaks scathingly indeed on more than one occasion of the *Dorshe Halaqot,* or Makers of Easy Interpretations, and most scholars are of the opinion that here the reference is to the Pharisees, whose rulings on certain Halachic matters were so lenient as to arouse the rage of the Qumran sectaries: but it is a commonplace of religious history for the most vehement polémic to be directed against those nearest in general outlook—not those furthest away, who precisely because of their remoteness may be overlooked. On the other hand, even if we take Josephus' phrase in the *Antiquities* quite literally, and assume the identity of the Zealots and Pharisees 'in all things' save that they had an inviolable attachment to liberty and maintained that 'God was to be their only Ruler and Lord', we must realise that the natural corollary of this apparently simple doctrine must have been the creation of a separate 'religious' body in the full sense of that term.

The sequences of events when the Zealots began their activities seems to have been something as follows. The people were restive under the harsh Roman rule, and revolution was endemic. None of the three then-existing religious bodies however took up any definite stand on the political issue. The Sadducees with their aristocratic leanings were mainly interested in the Temple cultus, the Essenes lived in seclusion, the Pharisees had a long tradition of political temporising and compromise and were prepared to submit to alien rule so long as they were allowed to carry on their religious and cultural programme undisturbed. The 'sophist' Judah the Galilaean, however, himself no doubt a Pharisee by origin like his colleague Zadok, elaborated a religious doctrine on which political discontent or even disloyalty could be based—that God alone was the sole Lord of the Jewish people; hence it was a cardinal religious sin for them to acknowledge any other rule, at all events a Torahless alien rule, in any shape or form or manner. There may be relics of this attitude in Judaism even today—for example, in the interpolation of the passage *Blessed be the Name of the Glory of His sovereignty for Ever and Aye* in the recital of the *Shema* proclaiming the Divine unity, and certain passages in the New Year liturgy in particular emphasizing the over-riding sovereignty of God over His people.

This doctrine was launched into practice in the year 6/7 C.E., when the Roman procurator Coponius imposed a poll-tax on the country: Judah the Galilaean now preached that the payment of this, being a recognition of Roman sovereignty, was an infringement of this cardinal religious principle of Judaism. The result was a wide-spread rebellion in the course of which he perished. His followers however, under the guidance of his sons (the youngest of them, who succeeded in 46, being considered like his father a 'sophist', or religious leader, as his two brothers executed by the Romans may have been before him) continued to maintain, propagate, and presumably develop his views.

We have the authority of Josephus that except for their basic doctrine the Zealots were superficially similar to the Pharisees 'in all things'. There must necessarily have been some differences in practice too, however slight, as will be seen later. But we must assume that basically the Zealot religious code did not drastically differ from that of the Pharisees—approximating to what today is considered 'normative' Judaism: they accepted at least broadly the validity of the so-called Oral Law and of the religious practices, developing those laid down in the Bible, which it comprised. In the opinion of the present writer, who considers the Qumran sect to have been Zealots, and therefore is inclined to use the Qumran literature to supplement our knowledge, there was greater strictness in some points—e.g., the observance of the Sabbath, marital and marriage laws, certain dietary regulations, and so on, as well as some divergences in calendar reckoning. But these (other than the last) were differences such as existed within Pharisaism, between the followers of one teacher and another, more exacting. However that may be, the important thing is that, in any case, the laws were meticulously observed, as they were by other Jews. There was no question of god-less bravos, as a cursory reading of Josephus leads one to imagine: the religious convictions of the Zealots were if anything more rather than less devout than those of other Jews, and their practices therefor more rather than less meticulous.

We have seen one Zealot *Halacha* that inevitably developed from the basic doctrine of the Fourth Philosophy: that it was a cardinal sin to acknowledge alien sovereignty by paying the poll-tax to the government. There is, of course, a reflection of this in a well-known anecdote of the New Testament (Matthew xxii. 15–22), when Jesus is asked, in the presence of Zealot sympathisers on the one hand and the government supporters (Herodians) on the other, whether it was or was not lawful to pay tribute to Caesar. However he answered, he would have become embroiled with one element or the other, and in a famous phrase ('Render unto Caesar') he evaded the issue, from certain points of view rather unsatisfactorily. In the course of the discussion another aspect of Zealot *Halacha* apparently emerges. The payment of tribute, with its direct acknowledgment of Roman sovereignty, was forbidden. But there were other actions which could be regarded as implying such recognition indirectly. Was it for example permissible to handle and to make use of coins bearing the likeness of the Emperor and the superscription that implied his sovereignty? Later on, in the third century, there were some pietists such as the saintly R. Nahum (Menachem) ben Simai who refused to handle such coins for other reasons, because they objected to the human likeness which they bore. But this consideration did not apparently arise in the present case—this particular objection seems to have become crystallised somewhat later—Jesus basing his reply on the assumption that persons who did not demur to recognise Roman authority implicitly by handling the coin with the Imperial likeness should not refuse to recognise it explicitly by paying the tribute. However that may be, here we have another, secondary, strict Zealot *Halacha* arising out of the foregoing: that it was sinful to make use of a coin the nature of which was an implicit recognition of alien sovereignty.

The immediate occasion for the launching of the Zealots as a separate sect was, we have seen, the proclamation by Judah the Galilaean that the payment of tribute was a cardinal sin for Jews. But this was not the only tax that weighed on Judaea at the time. There were numerous others, direct and indirect, such as tolls and market dues. How were these to be regarded? Some were for local purposes, some devolved ultimately on the government: some were exacted directly, some by tax-farmers and 'publicans', Jewish or non-Jewish. What was the attitude of the Zealots so far as these were concerned? Again, there was forced labour—for example, for maintaining roads or making bridges, which might be intended specifically for military purposes. What was the Zealot attitude towards all this? Some of it no doubt was considered permissible, much of it forbidden. But in any case, the 'sophists' who directed and inspired the sect had to come to a decision on these points.

There were of course many other problems to be considered. Might Gentiles be admitted to the Temple, even to the outer Court? Was it proper to offer sacrifice on behalf of Gentiles—a much-discussed question at the time of the Revolution of 66. The Mishnah (*Yadaim* iv. 8) records how a certain Galilaean 'heretic' (Judah himself, perhaps) argued with the Rabbis regarding the impropriety of mentioning the name of the secular ruler in dating a legal document (e.g., a Bill of Divorce) which embodied the name of Moses the Lawgiver—a natural point of divergence, as is obvious. We are informed by a late authority, the third-century Church Father Hippolytus, in his somewhat muddled work *Philosophumena,* that some Jews of his day ('Essenes' he calls them) refused not only to carry any coin bearing an image, but even to pass under a town-gateway surmounted by a statue (in some cases, at least, the symbol of the might of Rome): once more, a point on which the Zealot leaders must have given instruction. Again, what was to be the attitude of the Jew *vis-à-vis* the non-Jew as he went about his daily affairs? And what indeed *vis-à-vis* the Jew who did not follow Zealot prescriptions? The same Hippolytus states that the Zealots or *Sicarii* of his day would kill any Gentile whom they heard discussing (i.e. blaspheming: but possibly the writer is here exaggerating the Rabbinical apothegm deprecating the study of the Law by non-Jews) God or the *Torah.* We thus see that the very fact of the existence of the fundamental doctrine, that God alone was to be considered the King of the Jewish people and that the acknowledgment of any alien authority was sinful, inevitably led to the elaboration of a fairly extensive Zealot *Halacha* diverging from the Pharisaic rulings (always however on the side of severity) at various points.

It is obvious, indeed, that in first-century Judaea a man was compelled to acknowledge the Roman authority implicitly in one way or another at every stage of his normal life and activity—as he walked in the street, as he worked in his shop, as he toiled on his farm. There was only one way in which he could be certain of avoiding the possibility—and that was, by withdrawing from ordinary life and settling with other like-minded persons in an area where the Roman writ did not run and there was little likelihood of encountering either the hated oppressors or their minions. Hence, the establishment of a secluded 'monastic' centre, in some remote area of the country, was a natural corollary—if not for all Zealots at least for the more devoted among them, the *Sicarii*, who followed the teachings of Judah the Galilaean and his sons most faithfully and took up their residence on the Dead Sea Coast, at Masadah. Moreover, such a colony would have had to be closely organised, necessarily on theocratic lines, with a rigid discipline: there must have been rules of admission, of novitiate, of internal routine. Thus, whether or no the Qumran sect were Zealots, the likelihood of the existence of a monastic body among the Zealots, similar to the Qumran sect, cannot be seriously questioned.

Such a body would inevitably have organised itself to some extent on the same lines as other contemporary 'monastic' communities, such as for example the Essenes, which existed in this region at the time. In the natural course of things there would have been imitation, both conscious and unconscious, and superficially the two bodies would have had much in common. For similarity of organisational details even among warring bodies is in certain circumstances inevitable. We see it before our eyes, in for example the system of 'cells' used in our time by both Communist and Fascist groups as the nucleus for their expansion; and indeed there are parallels running through the whole structure of these bodies from top to bottom. Thus it is unwarranted to overlook the many divergences and to decide purely on the basis of the similarities between the data provided in the Dead Sea Scrolls on the one hand, and of Josephus, Pliny and Philo on the other, that the Dead Sea sectarians are necessarily identical with the Essenes.

The hypothesis of identity seemed, indeed, inevitable when the Scrolls were originally found in the classic Dead Sea region: and first impressions cannot easily be eradicated. But the differences, as they have emerged after a fuller study of the sources, are insurmountable and decisive. The fundamentally warlike Qumran sect of married votaries whose centre was liquidated by the Romans in the War of 66–73 cannot possibly be identical with the pacific celibates so admired by the Roman sycophant Josephus, nor with the gentle body (whose centre survived the War) lovingly described by the Roman officer Pliny, nor the quietistic group who never had any clash with authority (no place here for the central episode of the Teacher of Righteousness and his violent persecution by the Wicked [High] Priest!) delineated by Philo. Of course there may have been in the first century many shades of Essenism and near-Essenism, some of them merging into the various other religious groupings, and many Essenistic as well as Essene bodies and centres: and that the Qumran sectaries shared Essenic discipline in some respects, like the early Christian recluses, in no way conflicts with the thesis that they were actuated by the basic Zealot doctrine and followed in the main Pharisee or Pharisaic religious practice.

It may be taken for granted that a religious body in first-century Judaea would have expressed its outlook and its attitudes in writing, not improbably in the form of one of the pseudepigraphic works then so fashionable. Long since, Travers Herford, the Gentile historian of Pharisaism, attempted to associate the Zealots with the origins of the Apocalyptic literature as such, though later he retreated from his extreme view. On the other hand, various apocryphal and pseudepigraphical works have been ascribed to the sect: e.g. the Assumption of Moses, which looked forward to the redemption of Israel by those who were determined to die rather than 'transgress the commands of the Lord of Lords, the God of their Fathers': the Hebrew Elijah-Apocalypse with its remarkable name-lists: and so on. While all this is hypothetical, the fact that the Zealots are likely to have produced literature of this type needs no demonstration.

It was inevitable that the Zealot teaching must have influenced the teaching of the others—particularly that of the Pharisees, because of their general closeness in ideas and thought: partly from imitation, and partly as it were from competition, for sects can never allow a popular outlook to become exclusive to their competitors (as we see for example in today's universal awareness of social problems on the part of all religious bodies). The opposition to the hated Romans and rigorous avoidance of them which was basic to Zealot doctrine must have found great sympathy among all patriotic elements in the population of Judaea at this time. The pacific Pharisees could not adopt the basic Zealot doctrine, which implied in the long run armed revolt, but they tried to achieve the same result in another fashion. The 'Levitical' impurity of the Gentiles which came to be enunciated in more and more meticulous detail in the last days of the Second Temple, was perhaps the outcome of this.[1] The Pharisee, theoretically loyal to the Government, did not avoid contact on principle with the Army of Occupation and the inhabitants of the Greek cities, but he minimised it, in a manner which could not be stigmatised as 'disloyal', by extending almost preposterously the existing religious taboos. And somewhat later on, the 'Eighteen Ordinances', perhaps drawn up at the time of the outbreak of the Revolution, placed a religious embargo on the use of wine, oil, etc. of Gentile manufacture, thus cutting down even further the contacts between the two elements.[2]

To us who survey the scene from our occidental twentieth-century viewpoint, a basic difficulty remains in the way of thinking of the Zealots as a religious sect. How can the ruthless and bloody-handed political activists, whom Josephus describes, be thought of as a religious body, meticulous in their observances, and following a consistent religious philosophy and rules of life? Yet the two are wholly compatible, as recent experience has shown. It is notorious that the 'terrorist' elements in Palestine who were responsible for many bloody actions in the period 1946–8 were recruited to a large extent from the *Yeshiboth* and the highly-observant Oriental communities. And the scene at the height of the Civil War in seventeenth-century England (or even in America a century later) was in many ways not dissimilar. The Psalmist indeed had given the lead: 'High praises of God are in their throat, and a two-edged sword in their hand.' (Ps. cxlix. 6).

To sum up: although the basic Zealot doctrine appears at first sight to be political rather than religious in its application, its logical implications inevitably resulted in the emergence of a full-fledged religious 'sect', in the more specific sense: with its own body of doctrine, its *Halacha* and rules of practice, a corpus of literature expressing its ideas and discipline, and a dedicated leadership driven by its doctrinal outlook to live a secluded and quasi-monastic life. Notwithstanding the apparent simplicity and apparent worldliness of its doctrine, therefore, the Zealots were inevitably a Sect in the full sense of the term. It was a Sect, moreover, which at one time played an overwhelmingly important part in Jewish life. The significance of the action of R. Johanan ben Zakkai, at the time of the

[1] See A. Büchler, "The Levitical Impurity of the Gentile in Palestine before the Year 70" in *Jewish Quarterly Review* n.s. xvii, 1–81.

[2] I have dealt with this incidentally in my article, "An Ordinance against Images in Jerusalem, *A.D. 66*," in *Harvard Theological Review*, xlix. 169–177.

94

Siege of Jerusalem, was not merely that he secured permission to reopen the Pharisaic academies, but that he deliberately diverted Judaism as such from the heroic but dangerous path which it had begun to tread.[1]

[1] There are evidences of Zealot influences in Johanan ben Zakkai's own teaching, but he effectively suppressed them. The classical story of his greeting of Vespasian as Emperor when he was brought into his presence, after his escape from Jerusalem, implied perhaps (as also in the case of the ex-Revolutionary Josephus) a complete and public renunciation of Zealot doctrine.

Since the above lines were written and first published, the discoveries at Masadah have demonstrated how meticulously its defenders observed the minutiae of Jewish law, e.g. in matters of tithing. Josephus's picture of irreligious intransigents has thus been finally disproved.

APPENDIX J

THE CHARACTERS OF THE QUMRAN DOCUMENTS

The following is a summary of the characters mentioned in the Qumran literature, with what is stated about them. Sometimes the same person may be referred to under two slightly different characterisations (e.g. The Man of Lies and the Preacher of Lies) but no account is taken of this here. On the other hand, occasionally an epithet may be omitted when a person has just been referred to: e.g. the Wicked Priest seems to become The Priest immediately afterwards. Though this is assumed here, the differentiation is clearly indicated. No attention has been paid to hypothetical reconstructions however persuasive.

ABBREVIATIONS

D	Damascus Covenant
H	Habakkuk Commentary
Ho.	Hosea Commentary fragment
Ps.	Psalms Commentary fragment
N	Nahum Commentary fragment
M	Micah Commentary fragment
T.S.	Thanksgiving Psalms

Teacher of Righteousness. Has communications from God which are not credited by the Treacherous with the Man of Lies (H. 2: 1-3): is in opposition to Man of Lies but not helped by the House of Absalom (H. 5:10-12): told by God all the secrets of the prophets (H.7:4-5): belief in him will save those in the House of Judah who fulfil the Law (H. 8:1-3): for the sin committed against him and his counsel, the Wicked Priest will be punished (H. 9:4-7): is attacked by the Wicked

Priest on the Day of Atonement &c. (H. 11:4–8):(Teaches?) those who voluntarily join the chosen (M). The Teacher is a Priest (?) who built a community . . . (Ps): is raised up by God 410 years after 'Nebuchadnezzar king of Babylon' to teach those who know righteousness and to instruct the last generations what would happen in the last generation (D. I:11–2): arises in the End of Days (D. 8:12–3): the men of the Brotherhood (יחד) will listen to him (D. 9:20-28).

Teacher of the Brotherhood (מורה היחד(י)ד). Those who defect will not be included, between the time of his gathering in and the rise of the Messiah of Aaron and Israel (D. 8:35–20:1): it will be 40 years from his gathering in to the end of the warriors who went with the Man of Lies (D. 30:14–5).

Wicked Priest. Was originally called by name of truth (H. 8:8–9): after he ruled Israel he became proud, abandoned God, betrayed commandments for gain, stole, collected wealth of the men of violence who rebelled against God, took the wealth of Gentiles (H. 8:9–13). (The Priest) rebelled, and in retribution was tried by the wicked and tortured (H. 8:16–9:2): pursued the Teacher of Righteousness to swallow him up &c. (H. 11:4–8). (The Priest)'s shame greater than his glory: he drank the cup of anger and was disgraced (H. 11:12–5): was punished for his maltreatment of the poor and the simple ones of Judah who carry out the Torah (H. 12:2–6): performed abominations in Jerusalem, defiled the Sanctuary, stole from the poor (H. 12:8): sent (?) to kill . . . but was punished (Ps.).

Man of Lies. With the treacherous (does not believe) the instruction of the Teacher of Righteousness from the mouth of God (H. 2:1–2): publicly rejects the Torah, and is not opposed by House of Absalom (5:11): leaves with Men of War (D. 20:14–5).

Preacher of Lies. Misleads many to build a city of vanity in blood and to establish a community in falsehood: their labour will be in vain as they will be judged in fire to punish their insults to God's chosen (H. 10:9–13): preached falsely (D. 8:13). Mentioned (M).

Man of Scoffing. Preached falsely to Israel (D. 1:14–5).

Lion of Wrath. Smote with his great ones and counsellors (N.): hung men up alive (N.). Mentioned (Ho).

Last Priest. Put forth his hand to smite Ephraim (Ho). With his Counsel, the Priest will be attacked by the Wicked of Ephraim and Manasseh in the approaching time of trial, but will be redeemed by God (Ps.).

Last Priests of Jerusalem. Gather wealth from booty of Gentiles, but it will ultimately be captured by the armies of the Kittim (H. 9:12).

Ephraim. Attacked by the Last Priest (Ho): became ruler above Judah (?) (D. 7:13).

Ephraim and Manasseh. Their Wicked Ones will stretch forth their hand against the Priest and his counsellors at the time of testing (Ps.).

Makers of Smooth Interpretations. Invite . . . tros King of Greece to Jerusalem (N): persecuted by Lion of Wrath (N.): persecute writer of Thanksgiving Psalms (T.S.); the making of smooth interpretations will be punished (D. 1.18–19).

Absalom, House of. With their counsellors did not help the Teacher of Righteousness against the Man of Lies (H. 5:9–13).

Judah, House of. Those in it who perform the Torah will be saved from the House of Judgement for their belief in the Teacher of Righteousness (H. 8:1–3): there will be no further admission to it (D. 4:11).

Judah, Simple Ones of. Sentenced to destruction by the Wicked Priest (H. 12:4).

Judah, Wicked of. Will be cut off from the Camp with others who broke the boundary of the Torah (D. 20:26–7).

INDEX